'Susie Ashfield doesn't just tell you to f**king say it, she tells you *how* to f**king say it.'
William Sitwell

'Written with wit and style, this very helpful guide will enable anyone to deliver their message with real impact.'
Katrina Scior, Professor of Clinical Psychology, University College London

JUST F**KING SAY IT

JUST F**KING SAY IT

THE ULTIMATE GUIDE TO SPEAKING WITH CONFIDENCE IN ANY SITUATION

SUSIE ASHFIELD

ELLIOTT&THOMPSON

First published 2025 by
Elliott and Thompson Limited
2 John Street
London WC1N 2ES
www.eandtbooks.com

This paperback edition published in 2026

Represented by:
Authorised Rep Compliance Ltd.
Ground Floor, 71 Lower Baggot Street
Dublin, D02 P593
Ireland
www.arccompliance.com

ISBN: 978-1-78396-874-9

Copyright © Susie Ashfield 2025

The Author has asserted her rights under the Copyright, Designs and Patents Act, 1988, to be identified as Author of this Work.

All rights reserved. No part of this publication may be reproduced, stored in or introduced into a retrieval system, or transmitted, in any form, or by any means (electronic, mechanical, photocopying, recording or otherwise) without the prior written permission of the publisher. Any person who does any unauthorised act in relation to this publication may be liable to criminal prosecution and civil claims for damages.

9 8 7 6 5 4 3 2 1

A catalogue record for this book is available from the British Library.

Typesetting: Marie Doherty
Printed by CPI Group (UK) Ltd, Croydon, CR0 4YY

For Bol

CONTENTS

Introduction: How to Care Less — xi

PART 1: I ~~CAN'T~~ CAN F**KING DO THIS
1. The 'Con' of Confidence — 3
2. Kill That Voice in Your Head — 13

PART 2: HOW TO DO . . .
3. A Presentation — 27
4. An Inspirational Talk — 53
5. An Interview — 69
6. A Q&A Session — 85
7. A Meeting — 101
8. A Creative Conversation — 117
9. Self-Promotion Without Feeling Nauseous — 127
10. A Networking Event — 141
11. A Wedding Speech — 157
12. A Eulogy — 177

PART 3: WHAT ABOUT . . .
13. A F**k-Up — 191
14. Communicating With Difficult Creatures — 207
15. Asking for a Pay Rise — 225

PART 4: I JUST NEED TO KNOW . . .

16	How to Say 'No'	241
17	How to Disagree	255
18	How to Give Feedback	269

PART 5: ONE MORE THING . . .

| 19 | I Still Can't F**king Do This | 285 |

Bibliography	293
Acknowledgements	299
About the Author	302

INTRODUCTION: HOW TO CARE LESS

I reassure my client that his audience is piling in – there look to be about 7,000 people, the floor of the enormous stadium filling with shareholders and employees, day trippers and the odd journalist (poised to extract a sentence with surgical precision and repurpose it to tear the company apart in a witty, *FT*-reader way).

Though the client does not possess the charisma of Beyoncé or the comic timing of Peter Kay, he does have a message that he truly believes in. And while it might not be a message that everyone is longing to hear, he can deliver it without an autocue, which means everyone here will feel as if he's speaking directly to them.

My client and I are sequestered in a private room, hoping we won't be found by anyone wearing a headset or – worse – someone conveying last-minute bad news. And I'm watching the time. It won't be long before he's delivered onto the stage, which, with all the cameras and blinding lights, will feel as familiar to him as landing on planet Mars.

The client has gone quiet, which might be a sign of getting 'in the zone' (I have yet to work out what/where 'the zone' is) but more likely he's spiralling down the endless ways everything could come crashing down in front of him. I am primed to pull him onto dry land, playing out the conversation in my head. He'll tell me how the irrational side of his brain has kicked in. How he's gone from serene to imagining the audience yelling, 'Fraud!' How, right there, the company's share price will crash through stadium floor.

Without breaking eye contact, I say, 'Just tell me what you're thinking right now, James.' Pulling out a single earbud – emanating from which I detect Taylor Swift – he shakes his head. 'Oh, nothing yet. Don't worry. I'm just, you know, getting in the zone.'

James is going to do it. He's going to go out there and just f**king say it. But his zen-like aura in the face of what could have been unbridled terror hasn't arrived like some blessing from St Taylor. We've spent months in conversation, considered every angle – every feeling, every prop – to arrive at this moment. He will speak, and it'll sound as though something brilliant just popped into his head on the way to the stage.

I've yet to meet anyone who describes themselves as a 'naturally brilliant speaker' (and suspect they'd be bloody awful company). As with so many things in life, becoming proficient at public speaking requires grit, a willingness to dive repeatedly into the deep end. Sure, having a supportive environment helps, but embracing the challenge is half the battle. It continues to surprise me that the myth of 'great speakers being born like that' still abounds – the conceit that only a favoured few are bestowed with the gift of being able to speak in public, while the rest lose sleep over a five-minute client project update. In some it's so ingrained that they allow the belief that they're naturally poor communicators to dictate their career, actively seeking out roles that dodge the spotlight. What baffles me is that, albeit unknowingly, the very same individuals have effectively been engaging in public speaking from infancy. But the moment that a manager asks them to present a sales strategy to the team, they feel sick. If it was widely known that 'presenting' was just the same as 'talking', I'd be out of a job.

The difference between those who appear to be 'natural' performers and those who believe there's a chance they'll throw up before speaking comes down to a single factor: practice. But when I tell my clients that they'll perform better and feel calmer if they simply have a few run-throughs first, I'm met with disbelief. Surely, they think, there must be more to it than just that? Dolly Parton once observed, 'You'd be surprised how much it costs to look this cheap!' My equivalent statement is 'It's amazing how much rehearsal it takes to make a speaker look so off-the-cuff.' Speaking well, in any style, format or environment, can be learned, regardless of how unpleasant it might feel. And that is my job. My work ensures that my clients look good, sound good and feel good when they next have to speak in front of an audience. I am a speech coach. I will help you identify exactly what it is you want to say, then help you work out how to say it. I am the reason that when James's speech is over and the audience is leaving, I will overhear them say, 'But that's just *James*, isn't it? He's just a natural speaker.'

*

The following day I find myself in something that describes itself as 'The International Soho Business Centre'. In reality, it seems as though some wily entrepreneur has transformed the stockroom of a Chinese restaurant into a rentable office space, but it was the best I could find at short notice. With its cheap chipboard desks, peeling dry paint and faded posters, it's fair to say the place has seen better days. This run-down environment is in direct contrast to my extremely glamorous client who, despite her waist-long blow-dried hair, manicured nails and Chanel handbag, has tears streaming down her face. I dig around in my own handbag (not Chanel) and pull out a packet of Kleenex. She looks at me with mascara-stained eyes and tells me, 'I couldn't do it. After all the work we've been doing, I just couldn't say it. I couldn't say a single f**king thing!'

We've been steadily setting small tasks designed to gently expose her to the thing she fears more than anything: speaking up in boardroom meetings. In the past five weeks she's had two board meetings, and after both she's walked away kicking herself for all the things she didn't say. It's not that she didn't know *what* to say – or how to say it – it's just at the exact moment she wants to get her point across, her head is suddenly filled with a million worst-case scenarios that will never happen. 'What if I say the wrong thing?' 'What if I go bright red?' 'What if I go bright red and they all see me go bright red and they realise that I'm terrified and that makes them think I don't deserve to be in the room, and they all talk about it behind my back?'

We've spent hours discussing what 'the wrong thing' actually is, whether being publicly embarrassed results in a loss of professional credibility, or whether anyone even notices it. In all our conversations I'm trying to make my client think rationally about the root of her fear. Not in a way where we examine childhood trauma (some coaches do this; I'm not one) but in a way that makes her understand that the worst possible outcome of another person observing a flushed face is that they say, 'Hmm. That person has gone red. Probably because they're speaking in public. I wonder what time lunch is?' We've done the breathing exercises; she's tried hypnosis; we've explored the cognitive approach. There's just one option left. And if she takes that option, she'll win.

It's the advice that underpins this entire book. Seventy thousand words reduced to two words that I'm foolishly revealing in the introduction. Here they are:

Care. Less.

Care much, much less.

In caring less, you'll unlock the ability to just f**king say it. That is the essential premise of this book.

I'm convinced that caring less is the secret to the most successful people I've ever met. LinkedIn influencers will tell you it's resilience, empathy or a 6 a.m. ice bath, but it's this. *Care. F**king. Less.*

However, to care less you need to have three foundations in place:

1. Know you know your shit

Most people know their shit, but it's even more valuable to know you know it. You should feel as if you are good at what you do – whatever that is – to the extent that you don't ever feel as though you have to prove you know your shit to anyone.

2. Don't aim for mass likability

Be comfortable with the fact that not everyone is going to like you. Subjectivity is one of the core rights humans have, and if someone dares to take potshots behind your back, they're the problem, not you. Do your own thing and be comfortable that not everyone is going to love it immediately. Just look at the way high jumpers get themselves over the pole – it's inelegant and silly. This technique is known as the 'Fosbury flop', so named after Dick Fosbury, who realised that this style of jumping (alongside the recently invented modern safety mat) would give him the edge over his competitors, regardless of how much it caused them to snigger at how graceless he looked. They stopped laughing when he took the gold medal in 1968, and the once mocked 'Fosbury flop' became the widely adopted style you see today. If you stop yourself from speaking out because you're worried that a handful of people won't get it, you'll never change the status quo.

3. Try

Because if you accept points 1 and 2 without putting in any effort, then you're going to end up like the car-crash best man at a wedding, staggering from ex-girlfriend anecdote to ex-girlfriend anecdote. Knowing you tried gives you the same power as the child who learns early on that rosettes on sports day ultimately don't define you. You came last. So f**king what?

You participated. You didn't feign a headache despite really, really wanting to. That is true power. You tried.

If you master these three foundations of caring less, then f**king saying it will suddenly become second nature. Add to this the understanding that public speaking isn't something that the majority of people enjoy and you'll free yourself of the weight.

You should feel fear. It's a fact of life that sometimes you'll have to experience uncomfortable sensations. But think what you could achieve if public speaking *didn't* make you feel physically sick. What if you could speak up in any meeting regardless of who is sitting around the table? What if you could build a concise, compelling presentation in a couple of hours (as opposed to putting it off for months, then staying up until 3 a.m. the night before to compile eighty slides that prove you've covered every little thing)?

If you've picked up *Just F**king Say It*, then you're not just someone who enjoys rude words. You understand that real communication should be the North Star of your career, your life, your ambition. You understand that if you run towards something – rather than away from it – then you've put yourself in the driving seat, in control of your future. You have overcome anxiety. Most importantly, you'll be able to use this book like an instruction manual for communication, without having to do any kind of acting, exploration of your relationship with your parents, or even taking your shoes off.

Get ready to just f**king say it.

PART 1

I ~~CAN'T~~ CAN F**KING DO THIS

1

THE 'CON' OF CONFIDENCE

There is one client I think about more than anyone else I've ever worked with.

Before I met this client, the person who introduced us didn't hold back on the fact that I'd been brought in as the very last resort. She'd been seen by, I was told, 'the best in the country', and now, only out of sheer desperation, I was being put in front of her. Fair enough. I was twenty-six then and longing to appear older, more experienced and less desperate for work. I was chosen because she hadn't got on with any of her previous coaches, all of whom were male and significantly older than I was. And that was how it was put to me. She simply 'hadn't got on with' any of them.

Brooke Morrison was the rising star of weightlifting. When I met her, she had recently competed in two world championship finals and just won another title. While her sporting career went from medal to medal, her relationship with the press was less consistent, and her rare post-match interviews were mostly monosyllabic and emotionless. This was a problem for her agency, which had a firm eye on sponsorship deals and media contracts. Hence, coaches and media trainers had been called in, with little to show for it.

We were sent to a small, dusty office in West London that had once been a shop, somewhere that would provide neutral territory for both of us. Even though she was only a couple of years younger than me, I decided to dress 'up' to conceal my inexperience, making an effort to wear heavy, dark make-up, heels and a suit. At the last minute, I decided that a suit jacket might be overkill, so I swapped it for a cardigan. The overall effect resulted in me looking like a librarian going on a first date.

I arrived slightly ahead of time and dutifully set out notepads, pens and cups of water, ready to welcome in my new best friend. It wasn't too long before I heard a ping, and so I opened the door to Brooke, champion lifter and soon-to-be media sensation. I looked up, beaming. Brooke looked down and then down again. There was a tiny pause where we both took in the astonishing height difference between us. My height scrapes in at just over 5 feet, and Brooke seemed to be about double that, even with her slouching posture, which was accompanied by a profoundly unimpressed expression.

We must have run out of small talk – which consisted mainly of me firing questions at her about her journey and her responding with the words, 'It was all right' – after about three minutes. After an uncomfortable silence, I decided to jump in and explain the process, sticking rigidly to a script provided by the company I was employed by. Just as I was reaching a crucial point in my breathless monologue about putting the audience's needs ahead of the speaker's, Brooke's eyes went from the floor (where they'd been for all of our meeting so far) to her enormous black rucksack, from which she pulled out a phone and started typing. Alarm bells inside me began to go off. I am boring. I am bad at this. I cannot help her, and it is because I am terrible at the job I have only just started doing.

'Is everything all right, Brooke?'

'Yeah, it's all right.'

(Silence.)

'Does that make sense? The audience bit?'

'Yeah.'

(More silence.)

'Should I carry on?'

'If you like.'

So I carry on, and Brooke continues to gaze at her phone screen.

The panic in me rises. I cannot lose this job because it is the first job I've had in a long time that I actually enjoy, and up until today, I thought it might be the first job I had that I was good at. She is going to go back to her agency and tell them I was the worst of the lot. I look at Brooke with desperation, and she continues to ignore me. I can't remember exactly what I said next, but I do remember that I said it with desperation in my voice.

'Brooke, we both have to sit here and say we talked to each other for the whole session.'

'That's all right. I don't mind not talking.'

'Is that what you want to do?'

'Yeah. I don't have anything to say, really.'

'OK. If they ask, we have to say we talked and did some exercises.'

'All right.'

We sit silently for an hour, Brooke on her phone and me writing meaningless session notes. We did nothing, and then she left.

Unfortunately, our act works too well, and a month or so later, we meet back in the same room to build on the reported success of our previous session. From the look on Brooke's face, we are feeling the same way about having to spend another hour or so in each other's company. We settle in and Brooke pulls out her phone. I start doodling.

After what feels like forty minutes, Brooke is apparently bored of the silence. To my amazement, she shoots a question at me.

'Is this, like, what you do for a job all the time?'

'Most of the time. Sometimes I do voice-overs.'

'Voice-overs?'

'You know, voices for adverts and stuff. "Jersey Royals. Traditionally grown by the Jersey Royal Company. Simply. Delicious."'

She recoils.

'I didn't know you could do that for a job.'

'Well, I'd be shit at lifting weights.'

And now it is my turn to be surprised, because Brooke Morrison is laughing.

'You'd make a shite lifter. I don't think you could even pick up my lightest bumper plates.'

'What's a bumper plate?' I ask.

And suddenly, we are talking. And it turns out that despite being exceptionally different in every aspect, we do share one thing, and that is a sense of humour. Brooke is exceptionally dry, and we embark on a dark fantasy together in which my coaching sessions become so irritating to her that she reaches across the table and kills me with a single 10-kilogram barbell. We have found a broom in the back of a cleaning cupboard and we spend the rest of the time (which has now started to fly) with her showing me a few moves (snatch, clean and jerk, panda pull), perhaps to fill the silence or perhaps out of a genuine concern for my total lack of muscle mass.

By our next session, she is talking about the press, and I have abandoned the script. She tells me how she loathes the artificial nature of the post-lift interview.

'It was a f**king foul, how do they think I'm feeling?'

She's terrified of saying the 'wrong' thing, so her approach has become to say almost nothing at all. Her confidence can be so impacted by the inevitable interview that it has started to affect her performance in the arena. She has no fear of dropping the bar, breaking a bone or passing out, but the idea of journalists throwing questions at her that she can't answer is taking up more headspace than her opponents or her technique. Her argument is that her career should be driven by nothing other than her sport and that a champion is made on the platform, not in sponsorship deals. She doesn't need fans; she needs trophies. But Brooke is exceptionally intelligent, and as she says these thoughts out loud, I can see her connecting the dots.

I try to ascertain what she is frightened by. Brooke has this sense that the interviewers are trying to 'catch her out' but can't confirm exactly what trap they're setting for her. She's worried she might swear or give an aggressively short response to a question that she finds too obvious. She can't talk like a BBC presenter, she says; she hates 'acting'. And we agree that acting shouldn't come into it. Instead, I suggest that she should speak to the press as she speaks to me, which is a thought that she hasn't previously considered. We come to the conclusion that they're not interested in whether she says the 'wrong' thing or the 'right' thing – they just want her to say *something*. She agrees that in her next interview she will just say whatever comes into her head, even if that means swearing or stating the bloody obvious. A few weeks later I am sent a clip of her doing exactly that, while the interviewer runs around trying to think of more facetious questions to fill the time. To an outsider it might have looked uncomfortable, but at last Brooke has him feeling the pressure instead and she is the one in control.

*

'Just make me confident' is still a request I hear time and time again when I ask clients how they'd like me to help them. They're constantly chasing the word like it's some kind of holy grail, seeing it plastered everywhere, from political slogans to labels on deodorant sticks. But confidence is intrinsically linked to your own levels of self-esteem, which is nothing to do with me, and certainly isn't something that can be 'fixed' or improved in sixty minutes.

What can be achieved in that space of time, however, is coaching on the body language that will make you appear confident, even when that's not necessarily how you're feeling. If that's what you're after, then it's easy, and it's been written about many times before. You simply stand with your feet shoulder-width apart, push your shoulders back, make eye contact with your audience, smiling appropriately, using some deliberate and well-timed gesticulation, interjecting with frequent pauses. And there you have it! Confidence in a can. Apply liberally to the body every morning and wash off last thing at night before bed.

You can try this out now by pinching a few strands of hair from the top of your head. Pull them upwards and allow your whole body to follow, as if you're a puppet being pulled up by a string. Now let go of the hair while continuing to hold this position. This is how someone in control, someone who believes in their own ideas, looks when seated. Explore the difference in how you feel now from how you felt the last time you were hunched over a screen for a two-hour Zoom meeting.

In doing this you'll tap into a bit of a psychological trick, which is that no matter how nervous you are feeling, if you 'perform' these traits of confidence to an audience, they will see you as confident. In the same way that if you smile and nod at an audience, they will start to smile back at you (mostly internally, but often physically). Then the real magic happens, which is suddenly, out of nowhere, the nerves begin to dissipate. You look confident to the audience, they believe you really are confident, and you now feel as though you might have been that confident person all along. Confidence is not simply fake it to make it, but fake it to make it to actually acquire it. In a study from a research paper titled 'The effects of posture on self-perceived leadership', in the *International Journal of Business and Social Science*, it was confirmed that participants who had a consistently upright posture rated themselves higher in leadership than those who were slouched, and would even position themselves closer to the head of the table. In short, those who demonstrated body language that made them look as if they were in control felt in control.

The University of South Australia decided to test a similar theory in a study. They examined how a subtle smile (induced by asking participants to hold a pen in their teeth) impacted the perception of body and facial expressions. The results revealed that simply using the muscles required to smile (even if forced) were associated with feeling positive. Plastering on that smile ahead of doing something that terrifies you might not be such a bad idea after all.

In faking it, remember that you should not be aiming to play a character you are unfamiliar with. It should look like you, but it should look like whoever you are after, say, a pint and a half. I've observed that even my most austere clients lighten up once they're out of their glass-box room on the twenty-second floor, and into the Lamb Tavern. They move and talk organically, in a way that feels unguarded and engaging. This is the exact person they need to be back in that boardroom.

If you are looking for something more heavyset than a party trick, then it's actually even easier. Here is the formula for becoming confident:

$$(Knowledge + Practice) \times Experience$$
$$= CONFIDENCE$$

*

Knowledge. It is not enough to know your stuff; you have to know you know your stuff. At the time Brooke was speaking, she was not only a champion weightlifter, she'd also been the one on the platform, making her the world's leading expert on the question, 'And how did that go for you?'

You have competence. You have the required level of knowledge to do this. That's why you've been the one asked to speak. But you have to believe at the time you are speaking that you are an expert on your topic or, at that very least, you know enough to offer an informed opinion.

You must now blend this foundation of competence with practice. I don't know a single brilliant speaker who doesn't practise, and regardless of how great you believe your material to be, it won't make you feel at all in control if you can't reassure yourself that you've said this out loud a least a few times before you actually deliver. It's a simple premise: the more you practise, the more confident you will feel. For example, if you're giving a speech at a wedding, I'd suggest practising it out loud once a day every day for a month in the run up to the event. By the time you get to the day itself, you could do the whole thing standing on your head.

Finally, experience. Do not expect the great gift of confidence to pop up overnight. The more you expose yourself to the thing you're frightened of, the more you'll build a familiarity with it. In short, true confidence takes time to build. When you look at people who appear to be naturally brilliant speakers, what you're more likely seeing is someone who has just been more exposed to it than most. Experience builds over time, but it's the final factor in growing your self-esteem in the long run.

Take your base of knowledge, practise your delivery like crazy and, over time, the more you experience public speaking, the more confident you will feel. That's the real formula.

Whenever I think back to my early days of 'faking it to make it', I think of Brooke. We were both experiencing nervousness but were tackling it in two very different ways. I was trying to fake confidence through my aesthetic and Mary Poppins-esque cheerfulness, and she was trying to hide her lack of confidence through stonewalling. These tricks would suffice in the short term, but in the long run, it would be authenticity that pushed us through to a real working relationship.

I have followed her career closely and watch clips of her in interviews whenever they pop up. She is astonishingly natural, full of humour and depth. I have no doubt she's had plenty more coaching since we first met, but I like to think I'm the only one she's instructed in lifting.

My clean and jerk remains disappointingly weak.

2

KILL THAT VOICE IN YOUR HEAD

For just £220, easyJet can cure you of your deep-rooted fear of flying. They're not the only airline to offer a service like this, and whichever brand you opt for, there's a variety of techniques and therapies available, everything from hypnosis to neuro-linguistic-programming, to something suspiciously called 'The Jell-O Exercise'. easyJet's version is extremely popular and has a long waiting list, which is unsurprising given their claims of a 95 per cent success rate. The one thing that all these courses seem to share is that the final exercise is always a short flight. The optimum cure for anyone with aerophobia seems to have been unanimously agreed: sufferers must face their fear to push past it.

Contrary to popular belief, anxieties don't always come from some sort of childhood trauma. It might simply be the result of your brain trying to protect you from a worst-case scenario, which then becomes an unchallenged pattern of thinking or comfort blanket. Very, very rarely has anyone with a fear of flying actually had a near-death experience in an aeroplane. Instead, a grain of a thought has developed, unchallenged, over a long period of time. From a tiny seed of 'what if?' a flourishing, impenetrable dread has bloomed. It might have started out with those last-minute worries that we all experience: *What if the taxi/train is late? What if I forget my passport? What if the flight is delayed? What if they lose my luggage?*

These thoughts are, to an extent, helpful. Worrying about forgetting a passport has the likely outcome of you remembering to pack it. Brilliant. Your cautious mind has stepped in and prevented a problem. Great work, brain.

But for many, what starts out as a damage-limitation process can morph into something monstrous: *What if there's a delay? A delay from a storm? What if we fly in the storm? What if the pilot loses control? What if there's engine failure? What if we crash?*

And the more you spiral downwards, the harder it is to pull yourself out, until you've convinced yourself that the only conceivable result of you getting on a plane is certain death. Psychologists refer to this fixation on the worst possible outcome as 'catastrophising', and the sensation of purposefully doing things that cause you to feel distressed is often described as 'emotional self-harm'. The habit of catastrophising can become addictive because it can serve a variety of psychological needs, from offering the illusion of control to the avoidance of deeper issues, so your anxiety can feel strangely helpful or comforting.

As you read this, you might be able to laugh at the above thought pattern. You know full well that you have a lower chance of survival when you cross a road than you do on a flight. But this is almost identical to how someone with a fear of speaking in public might think. The moment you're told you're expected to give an update during a meeting, your brain identifies something that carries RISK. And so, in the same way, it kicks off a pattern of thinking that is designed to protect you. And it may start out totally rationally: *What if there's a tech issue? What if my information isn't something they want to hear? What if someone asks a question? What if I forget what I'm about to say?*

And then, it grows into an uncontrollable mess . . .

What if I forget what I'm about to say? What if I can't speak? What if I freeze up completely? What if my boss walks in and I freeze and I can't start speaking again and someone has to jump in on my behalf and my boss thinks I'm incompetent and they all start talking about me behind my back and when the inevitable restructure happens, they fire me?

Just as the fearful flyer has concluded that the only possible outcome of a flight is death, the anxious speaker has decided that the only possible outcome of delivering that monthly sales update to the team is total credibility loss.

The only way to prevent yourself from spiralling is to learn how to draw clear lines between where the logical thought is and where the irrational thinking creeps in. Do this by examining each thought and seeing how much evidence is behind it. Separate fact from fiction.

For example, someone with a fear of flying might think: *That funny noise means something is broken and the plane will crash* – but they have no evidence to support this thought. The only thing they really know (but are ignoring) is that every single flight they've taken in their lives so far has taken off and landed successfully.

Here's a diagram showing how distorted thoughts can take over a usually pragmatic mind:

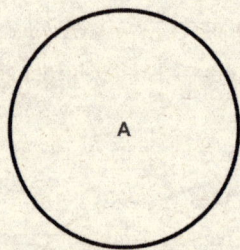

In this big circle labelled A is every presentation you've ever given. And every single one of those presentations has been 'fine'. They didn't set the world on fire – but they didn't need to. They're mostly just updates. They could have been better, but they could have been much worse. They were fine.

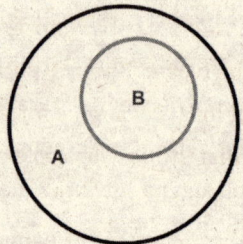

In circle B are all the presentations where it was better than 'fine'. It represents those occasional times where you really knocked it out of the park. You won the business from your pitch, you received great feedback, or you could see a tangible impact as the result of your message.

All of this is evidence. Actual, real-life evidence that supports the idea that, so far, all your presentations have been 'fine' or 'better than fine'.

But your brain has a convenient way of ignoring evidence when it's in panic mode. Instead, it focuses on this teeny tiny dot, C, here:

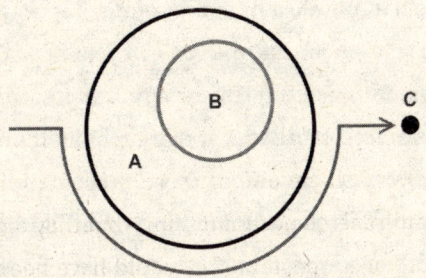

That dot represents all those distorted thoughts that keep you awake at night. And the more effort and energy you pump into that little dot, the bigger it grows, until it's completely overshadowed all of that lovely evidence for it being fine. You have convinced yourself that the only possible outcome of you speaking is the worst-case scenario.

How do you get yourself out of panic mode and back into the land of logic? You hold a mirror up to your anxiety and you start to pull it apart, piece by piece. If you can learn to identify that dot quickly, the faster you'll be able to see it for what it is:

a made-up but intrusive voice that causes unnecessary disruption. Psychologists call this process of identifying and challenging negative-thinking patterns 'cognitive restructuring'. It takes practice and patience, but by honing your ability to identify the thoughts that are causing the problem, the easier it becomes to challenge them. If you leave them wrapped up in a jumbled mess with all the other thoughts that you're experiencing, you might mistake them for another rational concern.

Think of the negative thought as a loud red parrot on your shoulder. It's a misconception that parrots can talk. They can make noises that mimic a human's sound, but they're not conversing with you – much like the voice in your head that tells you you'll say something outrageously stupid at your next meeting when you have zero evidence for that thought. It's not real, just an irrational concern squawking in your ear. There's no need to indulge it by thinking it has something significant to announce. Some clients have even found it helpful to give this parrot a name so that they know who they are addressing when they tell it to f**k off. The better you become at understanding real risk versus when it's just that bloody bird, the more in control you'll feel.

One client who was a partner at a law firm often heard her parrot just ahead of board meetings. Over time, she'd grown so confident about what she needed to say and how she needed to say it, her parrot had only one line left it could screech at her:

What if I shit myself?

Naturally, this had never *ever* happened before, but the more she thought about it, the more she felt that it actually might. This was easily fixed. From the moment she stated her concern out loud to me, she realised how ridiculous it was. After her confession, we sat in silence, both somewhat non-plussed. 'I have to say, that's not one I've heard before,' I said. After we'd stopped laughing, she shook her head. 'It's just not going to happen, is it?' she said. 'If it ever does, I'll give you a full refund,' I replied.

Everyone has these sorts of thoughts one way or another, but if you let the intrusive thoughts run the show, you'll find yourself unable to speak up when it matters, having to feign last-minute headaches ahead of presentations or read from a script in your next online meeting. Every time you give in to the intrusive thought, you give it more power.

Nerves are normal. Last-minute concerns can be a good thing. But convincing yourself that the moment you open your mouth you'll somehow cause your company to collapse is a sign that it's time to take control of your parrot.

The foundation step is to identify when the parrot on your shoulder starts making noise. Start to build awareness of what it sounds like and the sort of lines it comes out with. This takes time to master, but once you have it, you'll be able to begin the process of neatly separating your rational thoughts from the irrational ones.

Now you're ready to kill it using a technique of questioning that has existed since around 399 BCE, called the Socratic method, which the ancient Greek philosopher Socrates came up with in order to stimulate ideas and illuminate contradictions in an individual's thinking. Here we are, more than a few years down the road, using it as a core part of the cognitive restructuring process that will expose your irrational, negative thoughts.

Step 1: The moment you start to feel a familiar tightening in your throat, ask yourself this: What am I worried about?

The answer might start small: *I'm worried that I'll forget what I want to say.*

Fine, but dig deeper. How far does that thought go?

I'm worried I'll forget what I'm going to say, and people will see me freeze, and someone else will have to step in, and that will make the audience think I'm incompetent, and they'll all talk about me behind my back.

Now we have it. Sit with that thought for a moment.

Step 2: Look for any evidence or previous experience you have to support that thought.

It's important to clarify what evidence is and what it isn't. Evidence could come in the form of feedback, like a manager telling you that because you forgot how you wanted to end a sentence, they no longer believe you have any professional capability.

But evidence is not an assumption or a 'gut feeling' that comes from nowhere other than your own head.

Go through or write out each anxious thought. Put a line through the ones you cannot support with evidence. For example: *I will freeze, and I will be unable to carry on with my presentation.*

Unless you have actually had to stop a presentation midway through previously because you couldn't complete a sentence, then you don't have any actual evidence for this happening.

Step 3: With the anxious thoughts you have been able to provide evidence for, explore the consequence of each. For example: *I know I can forget what I'm about to say. This has happened before.*

Now ask yourself, what is the actual impact of this happening (again, evidence based)?

If I do forget what I'm about to say, there is normally a pause before I either have to start my point again or move on completely. Nothing else happens.

Write out the consequence of each anxiety.

Step 4: Be objective. Imagine a friend has presented this exact problem to you. What would you say to reassure them, based on the analysis you've just done?

If you do freeze, nothing actually happens. You just start speaking again after a pause, and you have no evidence to suggest that anyone will think any less of you if it does happen.

You have evidence to support the idea that every single time you have experienced a 'freeze', you have simply carried on with your presentation.

Repeat these steps as often as is necessary.

It might be helpful to keep a diary to address these anxieties over time, or you can quickly run through these questions the moment you hear that parrot kicking off:

1. What am I really worried about?
2. What evidence do I have to suggest this actually going to happen?
3. What evidence do I have to suggest this is not actually going to happen?
4. With my worries that I do have evidence for, what is the consequence of each?
5. Using the above analysis, what would I say to a friend who was in the same boat?

In doing so, you'll come to realise that nerves and their physical manifestations are completely to be expected. Your hands might shake, your mouth might go dry, but you'll be able to experience these sensations in the knowledge that there's actually nothing to be frightened of.

An aeronautical engineer I worked with to overcome his reliance on beta blockers to calm his extreme nerves ahead of presenting came up with a great analogy for this. He asked me if I'd ever watched the 1970s cartoon series *Scooby-Doo*. Fortunately, I had.

'It's the same show every week. Every week they're on the run from some crazy supernatural force, and every f**king week they take the mask off and it's just the janitor. That's exactly what this is.'

What the rocket scientist meant was that for years he'd been on the run from his fears, but now he'd stopped running to face them head on, he'd realised they weren't real. Now he understood that feeling fearful didn't automatically mean there was anything out there to be frightened of.

The feeling of fear is what causes your body to release adrenaline. The reason it decides to flush this hormone through your body is because your brain has sensed danger, and so this chemical helps you prepare to fight this perceived threat or run away from it very, very quickly (the 'fight-or-flight' response). If ever you feel that your mind sharpens up after a run or your heart rate increases during a scary film, adrenaline is what's behind it. Unfortunately, it often brings along a host of other symptoms that might not be useful for the actual situation you're facing – everything from knocking knees, feeling nauseous, a flushed face to shallow breathing.

Adrenaline is not only something you should accept but something you should embrace – it's likely to sharpen your focus, increase your energy and vastly improve your performance, in some cases even becoming addictive. This goes a long way in explaining why some groups of people actively choose to jump out of aeroplanes, while the rest of us are happy to remain seated. It explains why some people get on a roller coaster and think, *I'm going to die, this is terrible!* while others think, *I'm going to die! This is amazing!*

Why is it so many of us run from experiencing adrenaline, when it provides the same sense of euphoria and energy as class-A drugs without the adverse effects?

With my client, ahead of each small step we'd discuss what he was experiencing while contrasting that with what was actually happening. He might have felt sick, for example, but was he actually going to be sick? And if he was sick, how much of a problem would that realistically be? As he became more familiar with the symptoms of stage fright, the more he realised that that's all they were. Just physical manifestations of the negative voice in his head. Gradually, the fear factor went from off the scale to controllable, and then from controllable to exciting. In our final session he left with a question I was not expecting: 'What's next?' After rolling off a few corporate-talk opportunities, I realised the rush he was really looking for could only come from one place, and so I pointed him towards stand-up comedy classes that culminated in an open mic night and wished him the best of luck.

Anyone about to push themselves out of their comfort zone should expect to feel their heart rate increase. Accept that this is going to happen, but it doesn't mean that anyone is going to die, and you'll feel more capable of throwing yourself towards whatever it is you've been avoiding.

Facing the music is the crucial component, which is why the last exercise of any aerophobia course is the same: take the flight. Kill the parrot. March right up to the old janitor and tear off his costume. In doing so, you'll come to realise that you're much more in control of your symptoms than you've previously believed.

PART 2
HOW TO DO . . .

3

A PRESENTATION

A long time ago I worked in an office. I could never really believe that I worked in an office, but I did. I photocopied things. I made phone calls. I went to office Christmas parties. I'd never really planned to work in an office because after I left school, when my peers when off to university, I did what many might consider to be the career equivalent of buying a lottery ticket: I went to drama school. After three years of running around barefoot, wearing mostly black clothes and pretending to be other things, I graduated in 2010 in the wake of a financial crisis the likes of which the world hadn't seen since the Great Depression. There were stories of LSE graduates standing in the middle of roundabouts wearing sandwich boards, handing out CVs to passing motorists in the hope of employment. Ambitious alumni of Russell Group universities fought viciously for unpaid internships, and I was trying to get acting work, which meant I spent a lot of time waitressing. On one occasion, I ended up talking to a woman whose drink I was topping up. She suggested that

I'd enjoy working for her more than I would pouring out warm white wine at city networking events. In fact, she thought that I'd do quite well at her insurance brokerage. I agreed. Over the weekend I spent many hours discussing the proposition with my flatmates, and while we all thought the opportunity sounded great, we kept coming back to the same question: what is an insurance broker?

A few years in, I not only understood what an insurance broker was, I was enjoying being one. I had worked out that it was mostly about having lunches, and if there was one thing I felt I was proficient at, it was having lunches. I was in the role I was born to play. What had started as a temporary solution to covering my rent in between running to voice-over gigs for potatoes and mid-budget hotels soon became my full-time occupation. I liked the corporate world. No one told you that you were too short, too tall, too fat or too thin to be doing what you were doing. You were asked, encouraged even, to just get on with things. And so that's what I did. Time rolled on, and as it did, there was one observation that I kept coming back to. Corporate people, in my mind, were strategic, organised and professional. They managed companies and built trajectories and pitched ideas, and in order to do all of that, they communicated through presentations. Everything came down to these presentations, and yet, despite the endless sleepless nights they caused, they were always too long, mostly ineffective and consistently bland.

To me, this was the one area where the corporate world intersected with the performing arts – and most executives found it the hardest aspect of their job. It didn't matter whether they were the CEO or a trainee, they all hated it, they all found it to be hugely time-consuming, and they all seemed slightly afraid of having to do it. Occasionally, I'd be asked to deliver a presentation, which I'd relish. This drew attention, and I felt as if any moment my cover would be blown, and I'd be revealed as an impostor. 'She's just an actor pretending to be a professional – that's why she finds presenting so easy!' That was the line that I played to myself over and over. In reality, the result of my noticeable ease about standing up and speaking was that individuals who were senior to me would sneak over to my desk and start by asking if I'd 'cast an eye over tomorrow's slides', which became 'make any relevant edits to this script' and eventually, 'F**k it – you can just do it instead of me.'

I have seen thousands of presentations. Different subjects, styles, structures and stories, from hundreds of industries and a range of nationalities. I've seen an accountant ecstatically jump up and down over their koi carp collection. I've seen a roomful of graphic designers burst into tears after their colleague expressed how it felt to return to the office after chemotherapy. I've seen a software engineer deliver with the comic timing you'd expect from a night at the Apollo. When working with subjects that focus on human interest, adding in emotions and stories comes naturally. But when we're asked to deliver corporate information, we adopt a corporate style. It is completely possible to make the dullest of material dynamic, but we choose not to rock the boat. It's easier and safer to present a boring message in a boring way.

If your communication has a purpose, then it will always have the potential to be interesting. If your communication has no purpose, then why are you saying anything in the first place? Save your energy and send an email instead. Don't think you have to deliver at an Oscar-acceptance-speech level for the message to land, but if you want what you say to have an impact, then you have to follow two very important rules.

Rule 1: Know *why* you are speaking

Know exactly why you are saying whatever it is you want to say. This not only stops meaningless communication in its tracks but also ensures that you understand the objective. It takes a candid approach, but be honest with yourself.

For example, while an internal sales update might on the face of it be about bringing everyone up to speed, the true purpose might be to motivate the team to reach its targets. Or, if you're giving a talk to clients to inform them about a market development, the real goal might be to reinforce your expertise, encouraging them to send more business your way. Likewise, if you've been invited to speak at a fireside chat for a lively debate on one thing vs another, the purpose might not be for you to reach any kind of agreement by the end of the discussion but instead to inform and entertain your audience.

Clarify the true purpose of the presentation before you move on to . . .

Rule 2: Summarise everything you want to say in a single sentence

This step is the hardest part of any presentation, but the good news is, once you've cracked it, the rest will begin to fall into place. Start by asking yourself: *If my audience could remember only a single sentence in everything I'm about to say, what would I want that* one *sentence to be?*

The answer can be elusive, but keep digging and thinking and rewriting until you have it. Once it's there, the rest of the content practically writes itself.

Here's an example of how some very clever people might be approaching their presentation in the wrong way. Can you see how to apply the two rules above?

A group of medical experts is approaching a panel of venture capitalists with a product. Their product is a simple at-home testing kit, designed to be able to pick up various gene mutations, such as BRCA1 and BRCA2 (linked to breast cancer), through next-generation sequencing. The test is capable of sequencing thousands of genes or entire genomes faster and more cheaply than ever before.

Immediately, you'll be able to see how the key message could get lost. The scientists want to educate the investors as to how their sophisticated technology works because the amount of research they have put into it makes this the most important aspect to them.

The investors just want to know what the product is and how it will make them money.

Applying the two rules here would prevent the opportunity from being lost.

Rule 1. *Why* are we doing this presentation?
We are doing it to obtain investment.

Rule 2. What is the *one* sentence we need the investors to take away with them?
(I'll give you a clue, it isn't anything to do with how the gene sequencing worked.)
It is this: *This testing kit saves lives.*

If an investor knows a product saves lives – and will, therefore, be effective and in demand – they are much more likely to invest.

If the scientists keep reminding themselves of these two crucial questions, then their job at the presentation becomes immediately clearer. They can focus on what is important to their audience, not to them (as painful as that can feel), and ensure that they land that key message throughout the delivery.

It doesn't matter whether you're presenting something as simple as a five-minute project update or asking for a massive cheque: if you don't understand why you're speaking, and you can't explain what you're talking about in single sentence, you need to go back to square one.

How to Structure Your Presentation

After considering these two rules, you can move on to the next part of preparing your presentation: the material you'll include. Whether it's research, data, results, statistics, case studies or ideas, begin to pull together anything that feels relevant.

However, everything you gather should relate directly back to the answers to the two rules you've already put in place. If it doesn't, be ruthless and leave it out.

Once you've written down all the relevant points, you can start to structure the content. There is no right or wrong way to order your material, but the three most common styles I use with my clients are (a) a storytelling formula, (b) an informative formula and (c) the Q&A formula. This is what these formulas look like. You'll need to choose only one of them.

Structure A: A storytelling formula

Humans are hardwired to tell stories. We love a beginning, a middle and an end and have been using this same structure to communicate with each other for thousands and thousands of years. You can see it in ancient stories, from *The Odyssey* to *The Book of the Dead*, right back to *The Epic of Gilgamesh*, a Sumerian poem from *c.* 2100 BCE, widely considered to be the oldest story in the world.

Think back to the last book you read, the latest film or TV episode you watched, and you'll likely find it there too. Aristotle identified this three-act structure; German playwright Gustav Freytag remodelled it and called it 'Freytag's pyramid'; and later, Joseph Campbell, renowned mythologist, popularised it and labelled it the 'hero's journey'.

Freytag's pyramid is the structure I introduce to clients when we need a formula for a presentation that has a sense of progression through time. It's perfect for project updates, research findings or post-mortems but can also be used for 'big ticket' presentations when you need to entertain or inspire. A basic version looks like this:

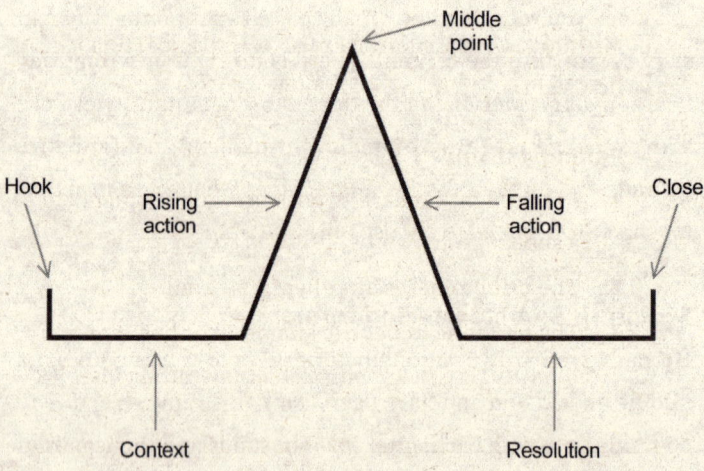

Here's how this works in story land:

Hook: Once upon a time . . .

Context: Cinderella lives a terrible life working as the servant for her ugly stepsisters and wicked stepmother. She dreams of a better future.

Rising action:
1   The prince hosts a ball, hopeful that he'll meet the love of his life.
2   Cinderella is prevented from attending the ball by her stepmother and stepsister.

3   Her fairy godmother appears with a range of practical solutions that will take her to the ball but expire at midnight.

Middle point: Cinderella meets the prince. It is love at first sight.

Falling action:
1   At midnight Cinderella flees the ball, leaving behind a shoe.
2   The prince chases after her to no avail.
3   The prince searches the kingdom for her, identifying her from impostors through a shoe-fitting test.

Resolution: The shoes fits! They marry. The stepsisters and stepmother receive their comeuppance.

Close: . . . And they all lived happily ever after.

You can see why the above structure works on preschoolers, but it's just as effective in the grown-up world too. Applying this structure to something as straightforward as a project update can breathe life into a message that might otherwise end up sounding pretty perfunctory. Here's how you can apply it:

Hook: If 'Once upon a time' works on a group of rowdy kids, just think what effect it will have on your audience. You can use a shocking statistic, a joke or an anecdote, but the opening hook has to grab attention.

Context: It's time to set the scene. Use this section to explain whatever it is you're about to launch into. This is where you explain the circumstances or situation that form the foundation or context of your message.

Rising action: Now you're getting to the meat of the content. Looking at the points you pulled out from your gathering material exercise, choose the ones that create a sense of progression towards the middle point. I recommend using three, because two is too few, and four is too many. Three is the magic number.

Middle point: Here's where 'it' happens. 'It' could be the be big reveal of the research, the moment where you encounter a challenge, or the point at which the bad thing/good thing you've been trying to avoid/achieve presents itself.

Falling action: Now that the middle point has revealed itself, you need to select the points that walk you away from it. Again, I'd recommend a rule of three. These three points might be the steps taken to capitalise on that opportunity, or the route back to the new normal, or the actions taken to meet the challenge.

Resolution: This sits in contrast to the context. Where are we now? What is the result or the impact? What lessons have been learned, or – if we're not there yet – what does the future look like? Conclude by summarising the journey.

Close: Have a line that closes the presentation. One clear, succinct sentence that encapsulates everything you want to say. It could even be a great place to directly say the one key message from Rule 2.

To see exactly what this *should* look like, let's use the example of one of my clients who has to debrief her team on a project. This client usually presents by building an extensive slide deck that she then reads out loud while wondering why something that should be simple overruns, lacks structure and regurgitates information that most of the room already knows. Instead, she could try this:

Hook: Six months ago, we set out to achieve the impossible . . .

Context: Our goal was to grow our customer base by 32 per cent, targeting Gen Z while preserving our brand's traditional identity, all under tight scrutiny from competitors and a tight deadline.

Rising action:
1. We rolled out a new social media strategy, targeting a large Gen Z audience.
2. Resource limitations and fast-changing algorithms quickly became a major hurdle.
3. Early engagement was promising, but we needed a faster pace to meet our target.

Middle point (breakthrough): We realised that we could repurpose existing content with a low-cost editing tool.

Falling action:
1. Repurposing content helped us stay consistent without overextending resources.
2. With a 'dice and slice' approach, we could react quickly to trends.
3. This strategy enabled us to keep up with platform changes and reach our target audience more effectively.

Resolution: We saw significant growth in Gen Z followers and surpassed our 32 per cent target. Repurposing allowed us to modernise our brand while maintaining its legacy.

Close: In just six months, we proved we could achieve the seemingly impossible. We should all be proud of what we've accomplished.

Creating content that fits Freytag's pyramid ensures that your presentation has a clear beginning, middle and end, encouraging easy engagement. You'll need to add in characters along the way, as well as setting the tone and describing emotional reactions, but by embracing the ancient principles of storytelling you'll go beyond merely updating your team and take them on a clear but compelling journey with you.

Structure B: An informative formula

When you need to explain, inform or instruct within a presentation, this second potential structure works effectively to give insight without bombarding or boring your audience. The story structure isn't as effective here as there aren't necessarily moments of peril, emotive highs and lows or even key characters. Instead, it's logically ordered, follows a sequential flow and encourages self-efficacy.

It's a style of presenting that isn't dissimilar to the iconic instruction manuals produced by IKEA that enable millions of customers around the world to put together flat-pack furniture without even using language. Just take the Billy bookcase, a product launched in 1979 that has become so popular it's estimated that one is sold somewhere in the world every five seconds. There were at least six of them in my first student flat, all of them put together with the guidance of one universal document.

Using this informative formula, we're going to follow a step-by-step approach to a shared vision with this presentation plan, outlining the project in question, the path and any potential problems along the way. Let's start by considering how those pragmatic Swedes might do it.

HOW TO DO...

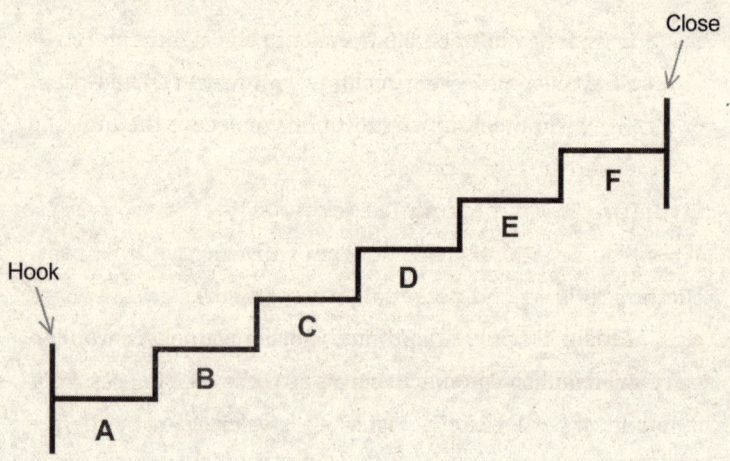

Hook: You have bought a bookshelf. Here is a picture of it.

A Before we get into the instructions, here is what you will need (a ruler, pencil and Allen key), who you need (a friend), where you should do this (on a carpet) and what to do if you need help (call the hotline).

B Look at the picture on the front again. Just to remind yourself of what it will look like once it's built.

C Now lay out all the pieces in front of you. Here is a picture of how they should be laid out.

D Attach this part to the other part and create the framework. Once you have the framework, start to screw in the shelves. Do *not* make the common mistake of installing the shelves upside-down.

E Slide the back of the product in and tighten it. Here's what that looks like in a close-up. Now you'll need to put screws in the following locations to secure the unit and ensure it stays together.

F Wow, look. You've made a whole bookcase. You're practically a carpenter now.

Close: It's time to add your books. Imagine how wonderful it will be when the shelves are full!

If IKEA can create a list of organised steps so clear that everyone from hapless students to ancient geriatrics can complete a building project, so can you. The key lies in providing clarity – covering all the vital details, without skipping steps, and consistently referencing the 'big picture' to keep your audience focused on the final outcome. Here's what that looks like:

Hook: As before, you'll still need a killer opening line to pull the focus of your audience immediately.

A Think about what the people in front of you will need to know or have to hand before embarking on the set of steps that will follow. This might include who the key players are, where the project is located and, vitally, *why* it is happening. Start by laying out these things here.

B Now outline the big picture. What will it look like once the project is complete? Clearly paint the vision and refer back to it throughout.

C Describe what is required for the first step to be put in place and lay out the specific elements of that first step in front of your audience.

D Establish the framework and outline the key milestones that need to be achieved across the project as a whole. Zoom in on the more complex parts and highlight any potential capacity for error.

E What is the next step? And the one after that? And then? Keep outlining what each step needs in order to be completed.

F Here's where you refer back to that initial big-picture vision and look back on the steps that took you there.

Close Choose one clear message to bring it all to a close. This is a good place to consider reminding them of the *why* of all of this.

Here's an example of how all this might work for a project manager who's been tasked with leading the company's mission to become carbon neutral.

Hook Our journey to becoming a carbon neutral company is about to begin.

A The CEO has asked this team to ensure our organisation becomes carbon neutral by 2030. We need to start now in order to meet that deadline. We are doing this to reduce our environmental impact and show we share the same concerns and values as our clients.

B We will become cleaner, greener and drastically improve our brand reputation as a carbon neutral company. Our carbon footprint will be lower, and we'll demonstrate environmental responsibility.

C The first step is to conduct an audit that shows us exactly where our greenhouse gas emissions are coming from at present and where we can make some serious changes. This framework will establish a baseline from which we can measure our progress. We can also start to make some immediate changes – switching to a carbon neutral energy company, incentivising greener commuting options and using local suppliers wherever possible.

D The next step will be to start using carbon neutral suppliers – after having investigated exactly how they are achieving that neutrality. We'll need to avoid tokenistic gestures, as we don't want to be seen as greenwashing and we want our impact to be real. After that, we'll investigate installing solar panelling to begin creating our own energy. There are bound to be complications along the way as we begin to learn more about exactly what is required, but I know that we'll be able to take a systematic and effective approach.

E We will also be embarking on training. We'll start by running workshops internally, then move on to educating our stakeholders. After that we'll implement policy to uphold and increase our green credentials as technology and circumstances develop.

F With these steps, we will become a carbon neutral company and trailblazers of our industry, ahead of 2030.

Close: We have an incredible opportunity ahead of us. A commitment to the environment matters now more than ever.

If this presentation is the springboard for a group discussion, you'll want to add in questions at each stage and check for agreement as you progress. You can either do this during the presentation if you're looking to facilitate a bigger conversation or save any questions for the end so that you can present the whole picture first before alternative routes are explored. If you're using this structure to host a workshop, then it's essential you give the opportunity for demonstrations and exercises throughout. The more interactive you can make the session, the more your attendees will learn.

There are a million different ways to present your information, and these two formulas won't work for every situation. Don't see them as being set in stone – see them as a guiding light. For example, you may have more than one reveal in a presentation, or you may find there's more than just three steps in your action plan. Be prepared to be flexible within these frameworks.

We have a final presentation formula to consider, however. And it's one of the easiest ways to cut through too much information and focus on what matters to your audience. If you already have a presentation in front of you that's full of tangles and needs some serious refinement, then the Q&A formula is one to consider.

Structure C: The Q&A formula

If you know what you want to say, but every time you open your mouth there's a landslide of too much information, work backwards by interviewing yourself. Imagine you are a journalist who needs to extract the key information under a strict time limit. What questions could you set yourself that would ensure you are forced to deliver the facts up front while weaving in examples along the way?

It could end up looking something like this:

Question: Why am I here? What are they about to hear me talk about?
Answer: I'm here to motivate the buying team to negotiate harder with our suppliers.

Question: What is my key message and what example do I have of it?
Answer: The key message is 'Don't ask, don't get.' I can use the example of my Italian factory visit last week, where we agreed a significant reduction on a new product line.

Question: What stats can I offer to back up my point?
Answer: If they all fight for an extra 5 per cent, coming up with creative ways to help enable suppliers to agree to this, that adds up to a profit increase of £1.2 million this year.

Question: What do I believe the positive outcome will be?
Answer: They'll feel more assertive in their roles, and our profits for the year will drastically increase.

Question: What story do I have to prove the positive outcome?
Answer: The accessories team did this five years ago, and the result was a huge boost to them and to the company.

Question: What (if anything) does the audience need to do next?
Answer: They need to sign up to the negotiations training workshops I've arranged for next quarter.

Question: What is the high-level overview of everything I've just said?
Answer: If we're able to push for just 5 per cent more in our negotiations with buyers this year, then we'll see an incredible impact overall. The team will feel more confident about negotiating and more comfortable about pushing prices down. The first step is to sign up to the negotiations training.

Using this formula means you can simply interview yourself within the presentation by putting each question on a series of little index cards, reading out the question and then delivering the answer to your audience. Practice is required, however, because each response should take up to three minutes to outline before you move onto the next question. You'll want to add detail and memorable examples. The beauty of this formula is that for a fifteen-minute presentation, you'll need to consider and answer only five key questions. It will prevent deviation, and you won't find yourself going around in circles.

How to Put It All Together

Once you understand your structure, it's time to get it on its feet. Transfer your content into a series of bullet points or questions and write them onto index cards. Then immediately start practising. Don't make the classic mistake of spending so much time perfecting the content that you don't get around to the speaking-it-out-loud stage because this is the much more useful part. The first few times it'll feel very clunky and disjointed, but keep pushing through. After the first two to three runs something promising and coherent will start to appear. I promise.

Now you're ready to add slides or images. These are the finishing touch and should be used only to enhance your message. Do not use this as an excuse simply to transfer your prompts into a deck. Bullet points, texts and graphs should be used sparingly, if at all. Follow the rule famously used by interior designers: if it is both practical *and* aesthetically pleasing, keep it. If not, change it or cut it out completely.

When it comes to the day of the presentation itself, you're allowed to take your index cards in with you. This isn't an exam. Remember, if you don't deliver the presentation exactly how you wanted, the audience won't know unless you choose to tell them. Once it's done, gather all the positive and practical feedback you can find and dismiss any comments that aren't pragmatic. Congratulate yourself. And start to plan the next one.

The Three Big Myths

Finally, here are the three biggest myths about presenting that you are going to confidently ignore:

> **Myth 1:** If you are given an hour to speak, you must fill that hour. You are there to fill a time slot.
>
> No one should be monologuing for longer than fifteen minutes, let alone sixty. A TED Talk, for example, is meant to last no longer than eighteen minutes, but even with the most amazing speakers in the world on show, I can't help but notice a correlation between the shortness of the talk and the number of views it gets. 'I Have a Dream' was seventeen minutes. 'When they go low, we go high' was fourteen, and 'We Shall Fight them on the Beaches' was just two. Going under time rarely, if ever, causes a problem, but overrunning can really create issues. This is especially true in online presentations when the audience will have an even more limited capacity to focus. If a manager or whoever has set the brief for the presentation tells you that you absolutely have to fill a time slot, stick to

the rule of monologuing for no longer than fifteen minutes, and break up the rest of the time with Q&A, group conversations or team exercises.

If you remember the experience of having that teacher at school who thought that reading a textbook out loud to you was the best possible way of teaching, then you'll understand how ineffective this approach is. My clients who have to train their audiences on a specific subject set up workshops with a simple formula: Explain, Demonstrate, Activity, Reflect. This ensures that they're never monologuing for too long and that they will receive comments like 'that went so quickly' from their attendees at the end of their full-day sessions. If you feel as though you're sitting back as the speaker and it's the audience that is doing the hard work, that's a really good sign.

Myth 2: You need to talk about the specific thing in the exact way you've been told.

I have heard many times the complaint: 'My manager just gave me their slides and asked me to stand in for them. I had no idea what to say.' Of course you didn't; you can't read your manager's mind. When this happens, you really should push back, but if that's not possible, ask what key message they want to land and then create your own material around that. That way it's still their message, but it's now your presentation.

While you need to stick roughly to the brief you've been given, it's your talk, so you have ownership of the content. If someone has extremely fixed views as to what you should be including, then why aren't they doing the talk? It's also worth noting that if you ask thirty different people what you should cover in your presentation, then you're likely to get thirty different answers. If you're the one being tasked with the delivery, then there's good reason for that. Don't even get me started on delivering someone else's slides. The result will be similar to wearing someone else's pants: weird, uncomfortable and confusing.

Myth 3: This is a test of your professional prowess and an opportunity to show how much you know.

If a book could make a noise, then at this point I'd want it to play that aggressive buzzing sound you hear when someone gets the answer wrong on a game show. A junior architect I worked with only ever had one objective with every presentation she ever gave and that was to justify to her boss that she knew what she was doing on every project and show him just how much she knew about architecture. The result was that her presentations were full of waffle, went on for over an hour and always opened with a strange elevator pitch that felt as out of place as it did egotistical. It's fair to say, the training institutions she was fresh out of had instilled in her the idea that the more she talked, the higher the mark her project would receive.

In the real world, this sort of approach will not only send you into a do-or-die mindset, it will absolutely guarantee that you end up overstuffing it. Less is always, always more, especially when you're standing in front of an external audience. If you can't explain your message in a way that would make sense to an eight-year-old, then you don't actually know what it is you're trying to say. It's only once in a blue moon that a presentation will come across as overly simplified, whereas presentations in which the speaker assumes that the audience has the same level of understanding as they do seem to be the status quo.

*

The more time I spent looking at other people's presentations, the more I realised that my time as an insurance broker was coming to an end. With a blend of hope and fear, I set up on my own.

Presentation after presentation followed. Conventional requests such as 'Can you run a workshop on confident communication?' came through, along with the less conventional ones including 'My Italian company is struggling to understand the body language of our new Japanese client. Can you please translate?'

It always came down to the same thing: that people are people, but the moment those people became an 'audience' was the moment they became an alien life force – impossible to predict or understand, and certainly hostile.

'I know I'm boring them,' says a speaker I've found fascinating to converse with. 'I just don't have the confidence,' says the one who's been presenting to their vast employee base for years. 'I'm constantly losing my place,' says another, who made their point with total clarity. Not a single one of them bothers to check with the audience how they're coming across, preferring to trust their own judgement of the situation. Speaking to someone who was in your audience would be like going behind enemy lines to my clients. They see it as a sneaky tactic likely to throw up false information that might deliberately send them in the wrong direction. Talk to your audience. They may have very different ideas, beliefs and desires from you, but they're still just humans, and all humans enjoy hearing stories, being entertained and being made to feel something. We far prefer the company of clowns to the company of experts.

I am frequently asked how I became a speech coach, to which there isn't really an answer. My truthful response is that I just started telling people that's what I was and, to my amazement, they started hiring me. A decade later, I wonder what would have happened had I told people that I was an astronaut.

I am still good at lunches.

4

AN INSPIRATIONAL TALK

'I think', said my client, 'that the world has probably had enough motivational talks.'

A small part of me agreed with her, but I told her what I always told myself whenever I was going to give a talk that was to be billed (from a pre-agreed set of objectives) as 'inspirational'. If just one person in that audience hears your message and it makes them do something different with their life, then isn't it worth it? She considered this for a bit, and then we carried on discussing all the different ways we could package her extraordinary story into a digestible, entertaining and – most important – sellable talk. It needed to be suitable for any audience, from a room of despondent teenagers to an after-dinner speech in front of insurance brokers and actuaries.

But we were struggling. Both of us knew it, and neither of us could quite work out why. I'd heard her tell the story a few times now, and the more I listened to the epic tale of her solo sailing mission around Cape Horn, the harder it felt to pick out the journey's climax – that crucial 'will-she-won't-she' bit. The trouble was, every single day was epic. There were so many highs and lows that it was tricky to choose the ones that the audience would really connect with. Even the simple act of heating up some dehydrated lasagne for a mid-storm lunch had all the surprises and heroism of a Hollywood blockbuster. Something somewhere wasn't falling into place.

Performing my usual trick, I'd revisited the purpose several times, looking for the metaphorical (or literal) anchor to the story. Why had she decided to go on this adventure? What had been her motivation? But she had a good response for this, and she'd paraphrase Kennedy's 'We choose to go to the Moon' speech, not because it is easy but because it is hard. This was what her father would've said to her, she'd tell me. Her beloved dad was one of those figures who'd lived a life so all-encompassing, his obituary had made it into a variety of broadsheets. He'd taken on hundreds of challenges of human endurance and been an exceptionally successful businessman and philanthropist to boot. In fact, our meetings were held in her father's former office, which now sat mostly unused, within the building of the company he'd founded. She had celebrity status there – I'd notice whenever we moved up and down the corridors, employees bustling past couldn't help but steal a glance at her. She'd often talk about him in our sessions but didn't want him to come into the material itself – she wanted to steer clear of anything that felt self-indulgent.

And so we'd continued plugging away at it, batting ideas back and forth at each other until we had the rough outline of something that had TED-style plotlines running through it. Unlike so many, she'd mastered her nerves and understood that adrenaline was just the sort of thing you should be feeling at the start line of any endurance test. Regardless, since her first delivery of the talk was to be to a group of sixth-formers in central London, I offered to celebrate with her afterwards, promising that I'd buy her a drink to toast her first performance. We ended up at The Cross Keys pub, the last true old-man boozer in Covent Garden. Children are the trickiest sort of audience you can get, which makes them the perfect warm-up challenge. But she'd been delighted with the result, and after a couple of drinks she confessed to me that there was only one part she'd 'cocked up'. It was the Q&A that had thrown her. She had been high on a blend of endorphins and relief, and when one lanky teen had raised a hand and asked her what had inspired her solo sail, she'd forgotten her tried-and-tested moonshot line, and instead she'd given him something awful: the truth.

'I just went off on one about the divorce,' she said, pushing one hand through her swept-back blonde hair, giggling. 'God. I've got no idea what made me do it.' This was the first time she'd mentioned the D-word, but suddenly a lot of things made sense, from the last-minute diary changes to the prominently placed pictures on her phone and desk, with the same three faces in it: one blonde lady and two blonde girls. I asked a couple of questions that must have felt to both of us as if I was tentatively poking the sore bit. I waited for the flinch, but there was no dramatic recoil. Instead, there was embarrassment. She dropped eye contact as she explained how, just one year ahead of her trip, she'd broken up with her husband of a decade, the father of her two beautiful children. Once the lawyers had completed all the paperwork, she found herself in a place she'd never been before: bored, angry, desperately hurt and full of self-loathing. 'The only silver-lining is that my father died before all of it happened. It would have devastated him.'

Here was a tale with more lows than highs, less gallantry, more desperation. To her, the word 'divorce' meant failure, and 'failure' was not a word that her late father would ever have used. It took some candid conversations before she believed that the truth was more interesting than someone else's justification for doing something, repurposed to fit her narrative. Part of her didn't want to share this deeply vulnerable side of herself with anyone outside her own private world, but with time, a new narrative developed. She agreed to ditch all the moonshot stuff and replace it with something honest. The solo trip had been fuelled as much by guilt as it had by wind. Guilt for her children, for her father, for the time she'd spent building a life that no longer looked like the picture on the front of the box. She was picking up the pieces of herself after a harrowing separation, desperate to do something that showed she still had an identity. She told herself that no matter how hard the sail would be, she'd do it. Not for human ambition, but because she needed to feel anything other than how she was feeling in the wreckage of her marriage.

The talk she delivered in the end felt less like a talk and more like one of those moments where as an audience member you are locked in a direct and intimate conversation with someone you feel as though you have known forever. She told me that on more than one occasion the room would stay silent for so long after she had finished speaking, that she thought they'd fallen unconscious – but then they burst into rapturous applause.

There is a reason we love clowns and loathe politicians. If you want to be relatable, tell audiences about your greatest failures before you tell them about your greatest success. The 'underdog effect' might be explained by social identity theory, which is the idea that people have a natural tendency to define themselves based on the groups that they belong to. Short people, tall people, nationality, gender, etc. We're constantly looking to connect with groups that we feel we'll be accepted by, which is why when we see Mr Bean try to read a social situation and completely get it wrong, we think, 'He's such a fool! He's just like me!' When we see 'thought leaders' tell us that they get up at 4 a.m. in the morning to do a full workout followed by a protein powder smoothie, we think, 'I don't want to be part of that, that doesn't remind me of me.' The anti-hero is always the side we'll connect with because they often act out of self-interest and are flawed and vulnerable – just like us.

Authenticity, despite what LinkedIn may tell you, does not come from your ability to be charismatic but your ability to acknowledge those times when you behaved like a shit. If you truly want to say something inspirational, don't tell the audience about your exchange with the Dalai Lama – tell them the one thing you'd rather no one else in the world knew about. If you want to inspire the audience, put yourself beneath them, and never above.

There are two types of inspirational talk that work. Either you have an incredible story or experience, or you don't. The first type is rarer, and while it makes finding material the easier gig, it is still possible to make the most extraordinary life event dull if you don't deliver the drama in the retelling. The second sort holds more of a challenge, but just as we all have that one friend who can turn a trip to the shops for chewing gum into a comedic saga, there are ways you can make something that the audience is already familiar with feel fresh.

The inspirational talk is not one you'll find yourself having to deliver every week, but you'll certainly have been in the audience for one – more than a few times in your life if you're lucky. On a low-key level, this could be the teacher you had at school who showed that they understood you, even when others didn't. That same teacher who valued your opinions as much as they did their own and pulled you aside one day to categorically tell you so, instilling a new sense of ambition thereafter. Or perhaps it was the weary team leader, who, in a moment of being kicked by both sides, spoke out to say that they understood the pressure you felt, the sky-high targets you'd been set, and how, despite all odds being against you, told you that they knew you were doing everything you could to turn it all around.

Sometimes it can even be the talk you just don't want to happen. A company that had built up a successful chain of hair salons in Liverpool called me in to work with one of its co-founders who'd recently taken on the position of CEO after the other founder had unexpectedly died. She didn't know how she'd step into the shoes of a man who had been the more gregarious of the two of them, often described as the 'father figure' of the company. She'd drafted a pile of notes, all now screwed up in the wire bin beside her desk, before resigning herself to the fact she'd just have to explain what she was going through – how heavily she felt the weight of responsibility on her shoulders, how guilty she felt at having to take his place and, above all, how much she needed his guidance now more than ever. Her words eventually landed as a raw mix of emotion and honesty. What else was there to say? Often, the most profound impact comes from recognising and giving voice to the feelings shared by those around you.

In each of these situations, the speaker is shoulder to shoulder with the audience and not above, as social hierarchy might traditionally place them. If you want to deliver a speech that inspires, don't believe that you have to talk about groundbreaking results, pioneering ideas or have a Hollywood-worthy hero's journey.

The three factors you need to add to any basic idea to turn it into something exceptional are: Difference, Tangibility and Stories.

Be Different

Unless you are in the privileged position of speaking about something brand new for the first time, you'll need to come up with a way of putting a new twist on an old trope. This doesn't mean you should drop balloons from the sky or do the whole thing while wearing a gorilla suit (unless you think this would actually be helpful), but you should be able to surprise the audience with a message they were not expecting to hear.

In doing this, you'll not only trigger an emotional response, but you'll tap into something called 'memory consolidation', which is when your brain replays and processes an unusual or unexpected experience as you sleep, setting it in stone somewhere deep in your long-term memory. This is said to be the reason we easily remember the big moments in life but struggle to recall why we just walked into the room we've just found ourselves in. Try this out now by taking a quiet moment to relax and take yourself back to an important birthday in your childhood. You may not remember what age it was that you were celebrating, but you may remember extraordinarily small details of the room you were in, the decorations on the cake, or even the colour and shape of a box containing a present.

Comedians will use the unexpected to create jokes that hinge on U-turns. A Rodney Dangerfield classic offers an excellent example:

> My wife and I were happy for twenty years.
> Then we met.

The expectation is that we're about to get a predictable reflection on romantic love. Instead, the surprise is that the relationship went downhill after the pair met.

How do you take a well-used theme, such as innovation, growth or leadership, and add a twist? An easy way is to look for patterns and then anomalies. What are the unexpected elements here? How could you take a narrative that appears to be going in one clear direction and then suddenly turn and go the opposite way? It doesn't even have to be a drastic change, either; small shocks work brilliantly.

For example, one client was giving a talk in a line-up of speakers at a graduation. He noticed that almost every single speaker ahead of him opened with the line, 'I'm delighted to be here today . . .' Picking up on the repetition, he took a chance and went with the opener, 'I am absolutely *not* delighted to be here. But you're also not paying me. So there must be *some* reason I've found myself speaking at my old school . . .' On a pretty dry afternoon, he experienced the biggest laugh of the day. Being different takes courage, but the pay-off is worth it.

Another client was asked to give a talk on leadership. She came to me with some excellent first drafts, full of valuable lessons on motivating a team intertwined with her own story of her journey to the top. It was a good talk, but we both agreed it sounded like every other talk we'd heard on the subject of leadership. We needed it to stand out and give an overused theme a novel edge, so I asked her to share with me all the moments in her life and career she hadn't felt like a leader. A riot of a list followed, entailing moments where she'd felt clear signs she wasn't destined for greatness, from being fired from a fast-food joint for dropping more burger patties than she flipped to accidentally cc'ing a group of senior executives into an email in which she expressed not entirely flattering thoughts about the then CEO. We suddenly had a series of stories that were not only totally unexpected but altogether more human and relatable. We laced these surprises into the talk and turned it from a cliché to a rollercoaster ride. Sometimes, being different is as simple as seeing the trope and deliberately steering into the opposite direction.

Be Tangible

If you can crack the trick of adding context to an abstract principle, you will be able to explain complex ideas to anyone you want to engage with. Charities are especially good at this because one of the best ways to motivate people to make a donation is to make the problem seem easily resolvable. For example, instead of saying, 'We're trying to get 119 million girls into formal education across the world', say, 'Three dollars a day is all it takes to sponsor Malia to go to school. That's less than the price of your morning cup of coffee.' With the first statement, there's very little there that contextually explains what it means in practical terms, and it feels far too big a problem ever to be resolved. With the second statement, not only does the issue feel easier to fix, but also much closer to home. You can use as much data and as many abstract theories as you like, as long as you then make them concrete.

A great example of this is in Hans Rosling's TED Talk titled 'Global Population Growth, box by box'. Hans Rosling is a Swedish academic, a physician and a genius, and he understands that if he wants to get millions of people to understand his message, he'll need to do it in a tactile way. He divides the world into four different income levels, each represented by a prop that he pulls from a plastic (IKEA) box. The poorest group, he explains, is saving to buy a pair of shoes (a pair of flip-flops is placed on the table). The wealthiest group is saving up for their next holiday (a toy plane appears). Immediately, the room understands quite how wide the gap is between the very richest box and the very poorest. The faster route would have been to use numbers: the average annual salary of a worker in Sierra Leone is less than $2,000, and for an American, it's just under $60,000. But unless you've lived in Sierra Leone and America and experienced both those salaries, then it's difficult to fully grasp the reality of that gap. The use of toys and boxes over graphs and numbers means that everyone in the audience very quickly 'gets it' – and is what makes this by some margin my favourite TED Talk ever.

You can make your point tangible with props or language or both. For example, people struggle to comprehend really large numbers – both one million and one billion sound so big that an audience might not immediately see just how vast the gap between them is. They could instead be presented in a more relatable way: 1 million seconds = 11.5 days (roughly); 1 billion seconds = 31.7 years (roughly). Or instead of telling an audience that it's been about 13.8 billion years since the Big Bang, condense it into twenty-four hours. In this context, humans have been on this earth for less than five seconds.

The roots of this lie in a very specific part of our childhood. Jean Piaget was a Swiss psychologist and teacher whose lifelong fascination with the way children learn led him to develop the theory of cognitive development. Piaget proposed that roughly between the ages of seven and eleven, a child goes through what he called the 'concrete operational stage', a stage where they become able to comprehend concrete information but still struggle with abstract concepts. This stage required a learning system that provided concrete explanations in order for the child to fully absorb what they were being taught. For example, in maths, the notion of fractions can be absolutely baffling, but all it takes is for one diligent teacher to introduce the notion through halves, quarters and slices of a pizza and the whole class suddenly gets it, and the world of fractions is opened up to them.

This is exactly where you should consider your audience to be. You understand your subject matter fully, but if you assume your audience has the same level of knowledge that you have, then they'll miss a huge opportunity to fathom the information you are giving them.

One client represented numbers of social media followers through grains of rice on a table, while another used a giant block of ice melting steadily in the background to symbolise the pressing urgency of climate change action, and one charity founder used a handful of oats to represent the amount a child under her care ate in the course of a day. These tools don't just make the speech a more memorable experience; they allow the audience to make sense of information that they previously had no comprehension of.

One of the aspects of my job that I absolutely love is needing to get an understanding of how an entire industry works from someone right at the top of that industry, in just a few short minutes. It is possible for me to go from one client talking about frontier versus emerging markets, to another client talking about the impact of a new drug trial in oncology, to (on one occasion) a client talking about actual rocket science. I have the privilege of sitting in the room with no more knowledge on their subject than a seven- to eleven-year-old would have, forcing the client to bring their subject to life for me using props, visuals and metaphors. The next time you are struggling to explain something, ask yourself, 'How would I translate this to an eight-year-old?' And see how this unlocks a more creative way of unfolding things.

Stories

I cannot think of a single inspirational talk that does not use storytelling heavily. If you watch just a handful of random TED Talks, I will put money on at least one of them starting with the line, 'When I was just x years old . . .' Case studies are the most effective way you have of winning over your audience in any piece of communication, from your next job interview to Oprah starting her Golden Globes acceptance speech by describing sitting on the linoleum floor of her mother's kitchen watching the television.

So why are so many of my clients frightened to use the sharpest tool in the box? Storytelling is the magic pill that unlocks something evolutionary, neurological and psychological in us, but for some unspoken reason, we see it as the sort of thing that is reserved for the artistic types, the type of people who enjoy musicals and bake-off contests. 'Storytelling is for children and fantasists,' we tell ourselves, and mentally draw a clear line between two boxes labelled 'work' and 'play'. Meanwhile, outside those two boxes, storytelling is inescapable. It's not just in books, theatre and films, it's on public transport, it's in your place of worship, it's plastered all over your screen as you endlessly scroll. Storytelling is the foundation of human connection, but as with so many things that should be blindingly obvious, if you don't look for it, you won't see it.

If you want to trace tales of the unexpected in your own content, there are a couple of ways to do it. The first is through exploring extreme versions of your subject. This doesn't need to be your own story, but it does need to be as outlandish as possible. I was once working with a director who believed there was no way we could draw out anything inspirational for her next big recruitment drive, not when her company was a group of underwriters. We looked at a list of everything that her company insured, trying to find the more unusual areas, and ended up looking at digital assets. Then we found stories by doing internet searches for terms such as 'bitcoin theft' or 'crypto scandal', and in no time at all, the perfect case study presented itself. The story that had taken up more than a few column inches in various news outlets was that of James Howells, a Welsh IT worker who, in 2013, had accidentally thrown away a hard drive that contained his carefully mined crypto. Howells was desperately trying to convince his local council to let him sift through the landfill site in the hope that he could locate the device, which was estimated to be worth around £227 million. Had Howell been insured through my client, he'd still be able to access his 8,000 bitcoin. Why use a statistic to inspire when James Howells' cautionary tale would go on to bring grimaces of pain to an audience's face?

The second, more powerful way is to look within your own motivation. What has bought you here, to give this talk that only you can give, and why does it matter? For another client, the CEO of a computer game company, it took a while to answer this honestly, as he was an intensely private individual. Eventually, he began talking about what drew him to online gaming, explaining that growing up with two parents in the military meant he frequently had to change homes and schools, resulting in a lonely and isolated childhood. Through playing online fantasy games, he had a consistent group of people in his life he could connect with. Using this as the opening story in a talk responding to the perception that gaming is destructive to relationships was far more persuasive than a statistic about how much time adolescents spend online. But he hadn't thought to use this extraordinary story in any of his speeches. It transpired he had partly seen it as too personal and partly too self-indulgent, but when he eventually decided to share it with his employees, he said it created a connection with them that hadn't existed before.

If you think back to the people in your life who really inspired you – a teacher, a friend or even a paid speaker – it is unlikely it was the message itself that stayed with you after all this time. Nor was it the rousing response of the waiting crowd. Ultimately, an inspiring message impacts you because it made you feel something. Those who can truly motivate do not showcase their own brilliance, resilience or tenacity. Instead, they share stories that empower their listeners, making them believe in their own ability to achieve more, fight harder and fly higher than they ever thought possible.

5

AN INTERVIEW

There are only two industries in the world that absolutely require you to wear a wig. One is the arts. From drag queens at The Admiral Duncan to titans of stage and screen, wigs are a major aspect of the gig. As I type this, Shakespeare's Globe is currently recruiting for a Deputy Head of Wigs, although, ironically, the role does not require you actually to wear one for the job itself.

The other industry is the law. Barristers and judges alike are still required to wear stiff, horsehair headpieces to reflect their status and show respect for the court. If nothing else, this adds a much needed sense of pizazz to lengthy monologues. It reflects tradition and legacy. It's old school.

These thoughts are repeating on me as I make my way to see my client in his chambers over at the Inner Temple. If you've never been to this mythical place in the heart of London, that's because you're not an oligarch seeking a divorce, a film crew looking for an 1870s backdrop, or a lawyer, judge, solicitor or clerk. If you are one of the aforementioned, then you'll be perfectly comfortable stepping through one of the heavy oak doorframes off Fleet Street and into a world where it is de rigueur to have a brand-new Mac computer next to your silver inkwell. Not that I can see either of these objects in the office that I have found myself in because the entire room is made up of endless towers of white plastic folders. Folder upon folder is precariously piled on top of each other, filling every section of the room, each bursting with papers. In fact, the only places where you can't see folders is where there's just loose bundles of papers, the folder around it having disintegrated many years ago. Across every single loose sheet there's an explosion of information – handwritten annotations, doodles and roads of highlighter pen running across the typed document. It is the perfect physical manifestation of my client's brain.

A clerk has escorted me to his office and makes the introduction to my new client. While Hollywood might see barristers as having the charismatic qualities that make them the subject of many TV series and films, for me, the clerks of chambers are more layered and enigmatic creatures. If you want to ensure that your legal representation turns up in the right place at the right time, wearing the right shoes, ask a clerk. If you want to know the romantic tensions, esoteric hearsay and temperament of every character in chambers, ask a clerk. And, if you need someone with a mental Rolodex that includes a person who could coach you though an interview that causes consistent bewilderment, ask a clerk. And so here I was, standing in front of my client, who was a barrister categorised as a 'junior' (despite his many decades of experience). In order to ascend to the next and ultimate level of his profession, he was applying to become a 'silk'. A 'silk' is a colloquialism for those who reach the dizzying heights of becoming a King's Counsel (hence 'KC') and work in the name of the monarchy. It also means they get to wear a shiny sort of frockcoat to indicate their status (again, some crossover with performers at The Admiral Duncan here).

Back in the day, an experienced lawyer might have received a tap on the shoulder to indicate they'd be receiving the upgrade, but these days, the more modern approach of the job interview is used, and that is where someone from an old world can find themselves up against strange and contemporary terminology, such as 'competency-based framework'. I am shown this framework by my client before I launch into the most boring interview question I can think of, and I ask him about his reflections from the last time he had to lead a team. Sometime later, we are wading around in the Indo-European etymology of the word 'teams'. We have passed through several court cases already, and I wonder how much longer it will be until the inevitable moment that I am asked to remind him of the question. We go through a couple of key points made by the judge on a case he won in the late 1990s first, and then he grinds to a halt. There's a chuckle, followed by an eye roll. It's almost a giggle. 'I've bloody lost it, haven't I? B*****. What was it you were after?'

I have seen this before.

Here is an individual who is having to break down his encyclopaedic level of knowledge into a tangible three-minute response. It is like asking him to condense all the information held in every folder of that one room into a sentence that would fit neatly onto a Post-it note. To explain the task back to him was equally challenging. He could not get his head around the idea that what was being asked of him was so astonishingly basic. Surely, this final hurdle could not be as simple as merely delivering examples that allowed the interviewer to tick off specific words and phrases from a list? There had to be more to it. Perhaps some references to ancient Greek tragedies would seal the deal? Or at the very least some Middle English literature?

As the day of the interview drew closer, I received an urgent message from his office roommate (who'd presumably been buried under a pile of paperwork all along). He'd been hearing some of the answers that my client had been rehearsing and was concerned that he'd drifted back into the twelfth century. I fired up Zoom and waited for my client's face to appear on the screen, beaming and bespectacled. This time, I asked how he'd ensure his commitment to his own ongoing learning and development. After just two minutes, we were somewhere deep in the comments of a senior government official on a complex environmental injunction, and it was time for an intervention.

'I'm going to try a different question now, and I want you to answer it as concisely as possible. Take your time with this one. Do you prefer coffee or tea?'

'Aha! I'd prefer a tea, thanks.'

'Why?'

'I'm a tea man. Always have been. Powers me through some of my hardest cases.'

'So it's a tea?'

'Yes. I choose tea.'

And then there's a lightbulb flash. His interview answers required no more information than this. Like a mad scientist who makes a breakthrough discovery that will lead him down a path of either evil or good, he pressed a hand to his forehead. A white plastic folder fell. Suddenly, he had it. I threw question after question at him, and the responses flowed, staccato-like and structured, each time looping in one of his spectacular cases to briefly evidence the answer.

Not many months after this call had happened, he was to take silk in some extraordinary ceremony that involves additional wigs and lots of bowing. He wrote me an extremely kind (yet noticeably concise) thank-you letter and recommended that I explore interview coaching as a professional career. To this day, I have no idea what he thought my job was.

I often wonder whether the more intelligent the client, the greater the challenge of a job interview. The idea that we have an iceberg of information within us and all that's needed is a few ice cubes off the top is unfathomable to many. Especially those who have expertise in an area far beyond their interviewers.

This phenomenon is known as the 'curse of knowledge', a cognitive bias that assumes the other party has equal levels of understanding to our own. Simply put, when something is blindingly obvious to us, we incorrectly believe it's blindingly obvious to everyone else. The impact of that is our communication becomes like a foreign language to those on the outside.

As an example of this, you can perform an experiment that was devised by Elizabeth Newton, a Stanford University graduate student back in 1990, to demonstrate the problem. Start by finding a friend with an open mind and a sense of humour, and then ask them to guess the pop song you are thinking of by tapping the song out on a table. Now watch as they are absolutely dumbfounded at the impossibility of working out what on earth you are tapping out the tune of. The magic of this is that you will also be flabbergasted by their inability to guess correctly, when the answer is so apparent. But of course, in your head, you're playing the song, aren't you? You can actually hear the music in your brain when all the other person can hear is a series of seemingly random knocks.

It reminds me of watching my father playing charades at Christmas. It is deeply frustrating to him that his audience cannot deduct from his taking of two puffs of an invisible cigarette that he is so obviously impersonating Camilla Parker Bowles. Who the hell else could it be?!

The thing is, for a job interview, the task is far easier than charades. It's as simple as having someone hum a tune at you, which you then just hum back to them. It really is that straightforward, because almost everything you need to include in your job interview is already in the job description. It's like being handed your final exam paper, with all of the answers accidentally stapled to the back of it.

Let's look at an example. Here's a job description for a shop manager:

> As the Manager of Just F**king Buy It, a clothing store, you will be responsible for overseeing all aspects of the shop's operations. You will play a crucial role in creating a welcoming and visually appealing environment while ensuring that the shop runs efficiently and profitably. Skills required include:
>
> - **Creativity:** Extensive experience in product curation alongside knowledge of market trends and customer preferences.
>
> - **Leadership:** Ability to effectively motivate and lead a team, delegate tasks, provide guidance and drive the vision of the business.
>
> - **Client management:** Outstanding skills in communication and an ability to resolve inquiries and handle complaints.

Step 1: Look at this job description really, really carefully. Pull out all the terms in there that are actual, tangible skills and put them in a list. For example:

- Creativity
- Leadership
- Client management

Step 2: Now come up with a real-life case study from your own career that matches up with that skill. For example, to demonstrate *leadership*, you'll need a true story from your own experience:

That time at work when we were unexpectedly short-staffed, so I had to step up and make sure everything still ran as smoothly as possible.

Note down at least one story for each skill on your list.

Step 3: Go through the stories and explain what happened, adding in detail. For bonus points, see whether you can use the language reflected in the job description. For example, in the section that mentions *leadership*, it mentions the ability to *delegate tasks* and *provide guidance*. See if you can add those in so that the story now sounds something like this:

That time at work when we were unexpectedly short-staffed, so I had to step up and make sure everything still ran as smoothly as possible. This meant I had to delegate tasks, *so that the team we had with us were able to easily fill in the gaps. I was communicating openly with them the whole time, so that they felt they were being carefully* guided *through any new task they were given.*

Don't forget to add in a 'happy ending' to each example, where you can add in the result, positive impact or lesson learned:

The team managed the day brilliantly, and we received amazing customer feedback.

You should end up with a list of stories and situations like the above, each reflecting a skill.

Step 4: Find some sample questions on the internet, an AI generator, or even in a book, and then select a few you want to practise.

Once you have a list of questions, you're going to practise answering them aloud using your collection of stories and an *Answer – Evidence – Answer* (AEA) formula, which looks like this:

Answer the question directly. (Keep this brief and just give a clear answer.)

Evidence for the answer. (Add in one of your stories here.)

Answer the question again. (Summarise and, again, keep it short.)

For example:
Question: Can you tell us about your leadership style?

Response: My leadership style has a strong focus on guidance and delegation . . .

(*Answers* the question directly.)

For example, there was a situation at work when we were unexpectedly short-staffed, so I had to step up and make sure everything still ran as smoothly as possible. This meant I had to *delegate tasks* so that the team we had with us were able to fill in the gaps easily. I communicated openly with them the whole time so that they felt they were being carefully *guided* through any new task they were given. The team managed the day brilliantly, and we received amazing customer feedback.

(*Evidence* for your answer using a story.)

That's why clear guidance and delegation are such a key part of my leadership style.
(*Answers* the question again.)

Keep going through the questions you've selected and answer each one aloud using the AEA formula. This is going to feel uncomfortable and weird, so if you have one, try to deliver it to your dog/cat. They're brilliant listeners and are unlikely to offer any unsolicited feedback. Practise and practise until you feel more comfortable with your answers.

Step 5: Brace yourself for some generic questions too, such as 'What have you been up to in the last six months?' or 'Why have you applied for this job?' or (everyone's least favourite) 'Where do you see yourself in five years' time?' No matter how blindingly obvious the answer might be to both of you, you still need to jump through the hoops. The AEA structure works well for these too, but you're also looking to tick three boxes:

- Here's why I'm great.
- Here's why this organisation is great.
- Here's why we'd be great together.

Example:

Question: Why have you applied for this job?

Answer: I have applied for this job because I strongly believe I'd be an excellent fit for it.

Evidence: I would manage Just F**king Buy It by focusing on the efficiency and profitability of the store. I'm doing this successfully in my current role by maintaining and improving client relationships and ensuring that my team are creating a great environment for our clients.

Answer: That's why I'd be a really good match for a shop that already has such an incredible reputation with its customers.

And if you're wondering 'Where on earth did she get that answer from?' The answer is, it's in the job description. Go back and read it again, and you'll realise I've just repeated the opening statement of their brief back to them.

If you are reading this and can hear yourself saying, 'It just can't be that fucking obvious, can it? To do that thing that has been keeping me awake at night for weeks?' – then you are not alone. I once worked with a highly respected gastroenterologist in Edinburgh who was being asked by the NHS to reapply for the job he had already been doing for eight years, and I can pinpoint the moment he had this realisation, session after frustrated session. You can understand his bewilderment. Here he was, doing the job he was perfectly qualified to do, and doing it well, and yet he'd been asked to attend an interview to reapply for the job he was already doing. It had the potential to bring about an existential crisis. You can also see why his mental response to this 'test' was to prove his credibility thoroughly and systematically.

When we first started sessions together, he'd respond to questions such as 'How do you prioritise caregiving in patient experience?' as if they were medical exams, using lengthy, complex terminology as though his interviewers were the highest level of expert in whatever '-ology' he was dissecting. It couldn't possibly be as straightforward as simply stating, 'It is important that patients feel cared for. Here is an example of what I did about an hour ago to ensure it happened.' But once the mental 'click' happened, he almost broke into laughter as he realised that in order to remain in his job, he just had to explain what his job was. Naturally, he got the job.

Some other dos and don'ts include:

DO:

Go in with a kick-arse attitude. Do this by visualising what it would be like six months into the role itself. I recommend this not for any kind of visualisation woo-woo but because it will help you talk confidently about what the organisation's brilliant future will look like with you in it.

Build rapport. Make it as conversational as possible. Do this by showing personality, flaws and friendliness. Besides, this is a two-way street, and they're here to impress you too.

Remember that they're on your side. They want you to do well, so they won't be setting any deliberate traps.

Think of questions you want to ask them. They can be as simple as: What does progression typically look like in this role? What does a day/week in this role look like?

DON'T:

Go in with a do or die attitude. If you put that much pressure on yourself, it might result in you over-explaining your answers or rushing your thoughts as well as your delivery.

Be self-deprecating. Not here, not now. Now is the time to shine a light on yourself because your competition won't hesitate to do that for themselves. It is vital that you highlight any successes by finishing as many stories as you can with a happy ending. This can be as simple as adding 'and afterwards I received incredibly positive feedback'.

Beg for it. There's a fine line between passionate and desperate. To avoid the latter, an unusual (but useful) trick is to go to a few job interviews for roles you're not absolutely gunning for before you go in for the one you really want.

Worry if you draw a blank. Ask for the question to be repeated/clarified, and if you end up feeling as though you didn't quite answer the question well enough, you can always come back to it at the end or ask to start your answer again. Just remain calm and be brave enough to stop, take a few steps back, and have another run at it.

Use passive language. Phrases like 'I think', 'it might/could' or 'possibly' have no place here. Passive language can creep in because we don't want to make promises we can't deliver on, in the same way we use 'we' instead of 'I' because we wouldn't want anyone in our team to go uncredited. Remember that the interviewer is interviewing you, not your current team. They want to know what you did/would do, so make sure that you're using 'I will'/'I know'/'It is' instead.

The Last Thing to Remember Before You Walk into the Room . . .

The job interview is not a test, nor is it an opportunity for you to demonstrate everything you know about the technical aspect of what you do. There's no such thing as a perfect answer, and you'll always walk away kicking yourself for that one small thing you forgot to say, but if the interviewer has heard their job description relayed back to them, they'll see a strong fit for the role.

If it doesn't land in your lap, you can ask for feedback, but don't stick a label on yourself that says 'bad at interviews' when there might be other unknown reasons (many of which will be totally out of your control) why you weren't their first choice.

Dust yourself off and remember that golden rule: care less. If they weren't excited by what you could bring to the table, go find somewhere else to eat.

6

A Q&A SESSION

It is November 2006, and at the annual Miss Teen USA, one shiny blonde gazes across at another even shinier blonde and, reading carefully off a cue card, asks Miss South Carolina for a response to the fact that (according to a recent poll), one-fifth of Americans can't locate the USA on a map.

Caitlin Upton barely pauses before she purses her glossy lips together and delivers an answer that would go down in history:

> I personally believe that US Americans are unable to do so because, um, some people out there in our nation don't have maps and, uh, I believe that our, uh, education like such as, uh, South Africa and, uh, the Iraq and everywhere like such as, and I believe that they should, uh, our education over here in the US should help the US, uh, should help South Africa and should help Iraq and the Asian countries, so we will be able to build up our future.

The YouTube clip showing her response currently stands at over 75 million views.

Some of my clients love the question-and-answer section of a talk. At last, they no longer have to play the character of presenter, and they can simply answer as themselves. It is not uncommon to witness a complete character change. For other clients, the Q&A is the part that keeps them awake at night. This is the section that is totally unscripted, exposed and out of their control. They believe that this where the real credibility test begins and the curveball questions will be thrown at them hard and fast.

While you are not expected to have the answer to everything, it goes without saying that you should be prepared. I learned this in a way that still haunts me to this day, when at the tender age of twelve, I had to be interviewed by the headmaster of a school my parents had hoped to send me to.

'For God's sake, Susannah,' said my mother, 'make sure you've read a newspaper before you go in.' The use of my first name in full meant she was being deadly serious, but naturally, being twelve, I ignored her. I remember sitting in an enormous leather chair and feeling as though I was passing the test with flying colours, responding to questions including 'Would you like to go this school?' and 'Do you enjoy learning new things?' with boundless enthusiasm.

Then came the curveball. 'What would be your short-term solutions for the Israel–Palestine conflict?' said the white-haired man in the opposite armchair. While I had heard these particular groups of words before, I had no context for them. They hung in the air in front of me, abstract of meaning. I paused. 'Could you repeat the question, please?' I asked. And he did. After the third time of him repeating the question, I knew I had to come clean. Everything would be lost now, so we might as well be done with it. 'My parents told me to pick up a newspaper before I came here, but I didn't. I'm very sorry, but I have absolutely no idea what you're talking about.' The old man threw back his head and laughed. Out of joy or pity, he then threw me an easier question (something about Tony Blair) and we carried on. To everyone's amazement, a few weeks later I received a letter saying I'd been granted a place. A short sentence had been added to the copy-and-paste document, commending my honest approach in the interview round.

If you go into any kind of Q&A session believing it is your sole responsibility to be able to give a brilliant response to every question, you are setting yourself up to fail. The point is not to prove your own genius, or that you might be exposed as – shock horror – someone who doesn't necessarily have an answer for everything. The same is true for meetings, presentations and first dates. Some clients tell me that if they become panicked by a question, they'll just hear white noise instead of the other person or get so wrapped up in their own internal monologue that they completely zone out. Regardless of any invisible social hierarchies that you may feel divide the room, anyone who asks you a question has done so because they value your answer.

Whether you are a panellist, expert guest or the host, there are a few things to do to ensure that if ever you're on stage and asked to describe your perfect date, you don't reply with 'April 25th'.

How to Be a Panel Host

Often disguised as a 'fireside chat', a Q&A session or panel can showcase a range of experts with varying ideas on a series of questions without solid answers. The one thing these experts generally have in common is that not one looks or acts as though they want to be there. Fortunately, one of them will silently nominate themselves the only one in the group who has opinions that matter and will bravely volunteer to answer all of the questions, talk over the other candidates and drive the session to a place so far away from the original topic that the audience will need a map and a compass to mentally return to where they started. Your job as host is to prevent this happening and keep the playing field level.

There is really only one rule that you absolutely need to understand. Here it is:

This is not about you.

This is about them. And that is fucking brilliant. You have the easiest gig of the lot. If you do 10 to 20 per cent of the talking, and the guests do the remaining 80 to 90 per cent, then you've been the perfect host. We've all heard those podcasts where the host talks over the guest so much, you wonder why they even bothered getting someone else on. Like the conductor of an orchestra, you are the one making the music happen, in almost total silence. Once you've understood the golden rule, there's not much else you need to do to ensure that it goes in the right direction. Other tips that help include the following:

Send questions in advance. You have your willing experts, but too much knowledge can be a dangerous thing, so ensure that they're aware of which pockets of their expertise you'll be dipping into. You don't have to send a list of questions that are set in stone, but the more indication you can give your guests of where you're going, the more they can prepare, and the more they'll sound as if they're enjoying themselves.

Have a list of questions in front of you but encourage an organic conversation. This shouldn't sound like a group job interview; it should sound like a group of fun people discussing something down the pub. In order to do that, you need to follow your gut instinct. For example, if you've gone through a question but one of the guests has an unexpected or interesting answer, don't move to the next question for the sake of following the piece of paper in front of you. Instead, dig into the response, and get the others to comment on it. Don't be fearful of the discussion going in a surprising direction – it'll be more enjoyable for everyone if you take a flexible approach.

Put in bold the key words of each question. That way, you can quickly glance down at your bit of paper and remind yourself what the next question might be without breaking away from the conversation. It also helps to keep things flowing and prevent it from feeling too structured.

Have more questions than you actually need. And tweak them as you go along, but always ask for an opening statement or brief introduction from each speaker, as well as a final takeaway comment.

Make space for the quieter guests. Politely pull back the ones that dominate the conversation. If you have one guest who's adamant that their voice matters the most, things are about to get really boring for the other guests and the audience. Bring more passive people in by name while respectfully pulling back the forthright speakers. For example, 'Sarah, can I just jump in here, because I'm really keen to get Raj's view on what you're saying. Raj, what's your take on Sarah's comment?'

Have fun. Seriously, enjoy it. If you do, so will the guests and so will the audience. Play with the guests if they're up for it, and build rapport with them. Don't be afraid to interrupt lengthy answers or push for more detail if you get the sense a speaker is holding back on the juicy bits.

How to Be a Panel Guest

A secret guilty pleasure of mine is being in the audience of a Q&A session, where one, just *one* of the panellists has something to sell (often a book). It will immediately become clear which one this speaker is. They will see the entire panel as a competitive sport, which they can win only by proving to the room that, of the assembled experts, they are the expertest. I never blame this person (especially not as someone who'd like to sell many, many copies of the very book you're currently reading) because it is the moderator's job to step in and, well, moderate.

I recently saw this at play with a panel of speakers who'd been brought in to talk about the challenges of being a female founder. The one speaker who hadn't actually had that experience was male, and he'd written a book on spiritual guidance. He'd almost certainly been selected because it was a guarantee he'd offer 'personality' to a conversation that hadn't really needed livening up in the first place. Jumping in with the line 'Well, actually, in my new book *Walking in Paths of Mountains*, I cover this brilliantly . . .' was quickly established to be the only way every question would be answered, but the highlight of the event was the moment when the guru decided to invite the audience to join a 'self-empowerment' exercise that he'd recently brought back from Bali. This involved asking everybody in the entire room to close their eyes and mentally identify the part of their body that felt the most 'empowered' and then, emboldened, to touch it. To a perplexed British audience on a wet Tuesday afternoon, this offer was as welcome as the idea of stripping naked, and so (with both my eyes open) I watched a room of obedient attendees use one hand to touch parts of their body they'd deemed as 'safety zones' – mostly heads and noses. Some of them had already turned pale in dreaded anticipation that they'd be asked to touch their neighbours' empowered parts, but regrettably, the moderator managed a hell of a segue out of the activity by asking the panel which of their funding rounds had left them feeling the most physically empowered.

If you think about it, being on a panel is a pretty weird experience. You travel all that way, answer two or three questions, and then you go home again. It might seem natural to panic about the pressure of those few minutes you'll be speaking for, but the only thing that should be of concern is if you'll miss your moment to get your point across.

It's likely that there is a mutual benefit to you giving your time to being on the panel, so don't squander the opportunity you have to raise your own personal profile or that of your company. Here's your golden rule to ensure you make the most of your big, brief moment. Before you attend the panel, ask yourself what is the one thing you'd like the audience to take away from your responses? Find a way to fit it into your answers. For example, if you have a company that sells luxury mattresses and you've been invited to talk on the topic of improving the well-being of office workers, you're going to want to make a point about the benefit of a good night's sleep. Link that to your product by explaining how your brand of mattress has been designed with that core benefit in mind. This is especially important, as you'll often end up speaking for no more than a few minutes, depending on the size of the panel and the abilities of the host.

Best guest tips

Don't be the person who talks over the other guests. If you find yourself saying something along the lines of 'Sorry, can I just add something here?' or 'So let me just jump in and say . . .' while someone else is halfway through a sentence, then you are that person. You're allowed to respectfully challenge a statement or refer back to something that was said earlier by someone, but make sure you give the other panellist space to finish their points.

Use the AEA formula for answers. Just as with a job interview, your answers should be clear, concise and simple, and should include some interesting examples. The most interesting guests on a panel are often the ones who can naturally insert case studies and short stories into their answers, so have a few up your sleeve ready to roll out. For example:

Question: What should busy professionals focus on when it comes to boosting their well-being?

Answer: The benefit of a consistent and healthy sleep schedule is fundamental to well-being.

Evidence: More than a few of our customers have told us that improving their bedtime routine had a huge knock-on effect on the way they dealt with daily stress.

Answer: Which just shows that if you get a good night's sleep in, it can really boost your overall well-being.

Ask for questions (or at least topics/themes) in advance and practise your answers. This is not cheating, and the host should be able to hand over (at the very least) an idea of what direction they want to take the conversation in.

Have a call to action. It is vital that if you're on the panel, you can give the audience some kind of way of connecting with you. Otherwise, you'll have gone all that way to give a four-minute response to a question before trudging home again. It could be a simple as your LinkedIn name, an email address or an offer to carry on the conversation with any audience members who'd like to after the panel has finished.

How to Answer Audience Questions

Here comes the moment where anything could happen. Whether you're opening up to the audience post-presentation or bringing them into the panel discussion, it's that moment you hear that fatal phrase, 'So are there any questions?' You could get some pretty reasonable questions, some absolutely off-the-wall comments or just a deafening silence. It can give you the same sensation of raising your head above the water in a lake full of speedboats. Some audience questions can be unexpected but interesting, most are entirely predictable, and some are batshit crazy.

From my experience as a speaker so far, I have two favourites. First, following a speech entitled 'How to Use Storytelling in Branding', someone asked the question 'So, how should I use storytelling when it comes to branding?' Some audience members just enjoy asking questions.

My second favourite came from an elderly audience in an unusual setting. During a luxury tour of stately homes across the UK, a speaker had become unwell and dropped out. At the last minute, I was brought in as a form of after-dinner entertainment and asked to deliver a talk on Debrett's, a publishing company and authority on the British aristocracy. After a brief presentation that included the correct pronunciation and dissection of a scone, we came to the Q&A. Immediately, a spritely octogenarian shot up her hand. She described a case study in which Lady Arabella Blackthorn encounters Lady Claudia Fairweather. She demanded to know which of the two should have greater status in the room, giving additional details, such as the age of their titles and their very, very distant positioning to the throne. I had not been prepared for this. While I sat, open mouthed, the cogs frantically turning, the butler, or at least a man who had been brought in to be the butler for the week, stepped in and explained exactly why Lady Blackthorn would absolutely have had the higher ranking and, therefore, be addressed first. Later, I went to thank him profusely for his save. He turned out to be an actor. 'The thing is,' he said, 'I'm not honestly sure that I gave the correct answer. I just said the thing I suspected Lady Blackthorn wanted to hear.'

Having had her superior position in the aristocracy confirmed back to her by an 'expert', Lady Blackthorn gave a glowing review of the entire event, and I gained an insight into how it feels when a question is thrown at you with a hidden agenda. You might feel as though your knowledge is being tested when, in reality, it's not your expertise that's being judged. That may go some way to explaining why speakers are often presented with comments that don't have a question in them. What is happening is that the question-asker just wants to feel included in the conversation, and all you need to do in that moment is offer them a brief moment of validation.

Here are some tips on how to reply when you don't know the answer, or there isn't an answer, or even a question:

1 **Ask the asker.** Just like Lady Blackthorn, there's a chance your question-asker might already know the answer or have a strong opinion on what they'd like it to be. If the question seems just a bit too specific, ask them for their opinion. Then have a mental rest for two minutes while they answer their own question.

2 **Ask the audience.** If you're running a workshop or think that the answer could be easily polled, have the audacity to throw the answer out to the crowd. For example, if someone asks if you believe that AI is going to massively disrupt your industry, and you just so happen to have a body of industry leaders in front of you, why not get them to stick their hands up to indicate whether they agree with the statement or

not. It's an easy exercise to run and produces a useful springboard for a wider conversation.

3. **Ask the expert.** If you know you happen to have someone in the room who's better placed than you are to give an answer, hand it to them. Your objective with any question is to get the best possible answer back to the asker, and this will do exactly that. Make sure they'll be happy to answer on your behalf first though. You don't want to be accused of throwing a colleague under a bus . . .

4. **Ask them to clarify the question.** If you get a question that seems a bit garbled or convoluted, it's a likely sign that the asker is nervous. Go back and forth with them until you have shaped something that you can give an answer to. They always appreciate it, and it makes it much easier for you to respond.

5. **If it's a speculative question, speculate.** With questions where there's no solid answer, you're just being asked to comment on what you think will happen. Nobody is going to hunt you down in a few years if your prediction wasn't accurate, but you're welcome to acknowledge that you can't give an answer that is guaranteed to be correct. For example, when I'm asked how much I think AI will impact speech coaches and writers, I will often open my response with 'To be honest with you, I have no idea. But I think

from what I've seen so far that what I believe will happen is...'

6 **If you need to think about it, think about it.**
You are welcome to say, 'That's a really interesting question' to buy time, as long as you don't overuse the phrase. It's better to go with 'Let me just think about that for a second.' It feels more authentic.

7 **Say 'I don't know, let me get back to you on that'.**
If you do not know the answer to something, you can say, 'I don't know.' You will not lose credibility in doing so. If anything, you'll gain a huge amount of respect for having the balls to admit it. I'd choose a line like 'I don't actually have that information readily available right now. I wouldn't want to give you an answer that wasn't correct so if you can hold on until I'm back at my desk I can get you an accurate response.'

The only thing you should never, ever, ever do is make it up, or lie, even if you're on the spot. Just look at any politician or [cough] member of the Royal Family who's been caught out by a journalist who's quick with the maths or has looked into the facts. You will come to regret it.

*

Way back in 2007, Miss South Carolina was mocked all around the world for answering a question in a way that was not just meandering but completely nonsensical. The internet had found its next victim in the teenage beauty queen, and if there's one group of people out there we love to hate, pageant contestants are somewhere at the top of the list. What you might not have seen, however, is what happened next. Upton was invited on to *The Today Show*, where her sympathetic hosts give her a second shot at answering the same question.

> Well, personally, my friends and I, we know exactly where the United States is on our map. I don't know anyone else who doesn't. And if the statistics are correct, I believe that there should be more emphasis on geography.

Given another chance, she succinctly expresses the sentiment that she'd been holding back on – who the hell can't find America on a map? But that's the problem with beauty pageants. They're formulaic, glossy and artificial. And in that kind of environment, any question asked is absolutely going to result in a disingenuous answer. Play stupid games, win stupid prizes.

By her own admission, she panicked. She was just eighteen years old when the statistic was thrown at her, and it was her first time on national television. 'I was overwhelmed,' she explained. 'I was in complete shock . . . I seriously think I only heard one or two words of the actual question itself.'

Remember that unless you are in a beauty pageant, a Q&A session is not a test. When someone asks you a question, most of the time it's because they believe you have something interesting to offer in response. You are allowed to go back and forth with the question-asker until you have clarified exactly what they are wanting to hear from you. You have more than one chance to calmly review and reply. As ever, the best way to do this is with unrestrained honesty.

Caitlin Upton finished fourth in the competition and went on to have a successful modelling career before becoming a realtor. I often wonder what the impact would have been had she answered in a way of a typical teenager, without the cameras, the lights or the tiara. I imagine her saying what it feels as if she wanted to say all along: 'Wow, seriously? Well, I guess some people just don't own maps.'

7

A MEETING

Right now, all over the world, millions of people are sitting in a room somewhere, thinking the same thing: 'This meeting could have been an email.'

And they're not wrong. It could have been an email, a direct message or even a phone call, but ever since humans learned how to use language, they've also known that the solution to boredom, loneliness or a desperate lack of attention is to hold a meeting. Technology has made this new global pandemic worse, causing physical symptoms we'd normally associate with horrible ailments. If you've ever seen that friend who emerges out from behind a screen, bleary-eyed, aching and grey, then you'll recognise all the signs of it, even before they apologetically mumble, 'I've just had a day of back-to-back Zoom calls . . .'

Brilliant meetings do happen. They are a fundamental part of our lives and should come so naturally to us – after all, they're essentially just conversations but with structure. They're the best and most efficient way for us to progress, collaborate and align. So why are so many of them going wrong? And how do we avoid it?

More often than not, it's a combination of gathering the wrong people in the wrong place at the wrong time.

Sometimes, as both hosts and participants in meetings, we can start listening to all the insecurities that rattle around in our heads. And as we begin to see meetings as an opportunity to protect or promote our professional reputation, we focus more on those aspects than on how to collectively reach the best possible outcome.

Here's an example of a meeting where the head gremlins are running the show:

> Claudia – Managing Director of Pop & Cork Marketing
> Caroline – Client Manager
> Eva, Tom, Sven – Caroline's Team
> Greg – Intern
> Chen – External Consultant

Claudia is the managing director of Pop & Cork Marketing. She has called a meeting to discuss their latest client: Pup Sup, a luxury pet-food company that needs to promote its latest outlandish product – a carbonated, gravy-flavoured drink suitable for dogs, called Cham-paw. Claudia wants an update on how the project is going, so she calls a meeting.

She's asked Caroline, the client manager, to arrange it. Caroline has chosen to bring along the people in her team who seem to be doing most of the work for the client: Eva, Tom and Sven. She's also brought the intern along so that Greg can be exposed to more internal meetings. There's an external consultant called Chen who's been called in to help with the branding of the project, so naturally, she's been invited along (last minute) too.

The meeting starts. Claudia doesn't waste time and immediately hands over to Caroline, inviting her to 'dive right in'. Caroline embarks on an engaging monologue, telling the story of how they won the client. Greg (the intern) listens along and nods intently. There's less of a reaction from the rest of the group because they already know this part. Just before Caroline reaches the bit that explains exactly where the project is now, she hands over to rest of the room and hopes that someone else will jump in.

Fortunately, Tom does. He has identified a couple of problem areas that he'd like to discuss, but Sven cuts him off halfway into his second problem because he thinks Tom's misread the client, and he's built a list of objectives that are out of sync with theirs. The whole room sits back and watches this Tom vs Sven debate continue for some time.

Fortunately, their increasingly lively discussion is interrupted by Chen the consultant turning up, seventeen minutes after the meeting has started. She apologises for the disruption and immediately launches into a branding update for Cham-paw, explaining the predicament she's been facing with the client. They want a logo that reflects their current branding style, but she's been trying to convince them that they need to go in a new direction. Greg nods intently again. He can see why that would be a problem. Eva continues to say nothing.

Once Chen has finished her update, Sven explains to Tom why the points Chen has just made perfectly reflect what he was trying to explain only moments ago. Claudia realises the meeting is now overrunning by about fifteen minutes, so she asks Caroline to get a summary back to her later. Caroline responds by offering her take on the Tom vs Sven debate, before acknowledging that a summary of the discussion would be helpful. Chen asks to be 'looped in on that'. Caroline offers her one better – a follow-up meeting next week to 'dig in' to the client's objectives. Everyone agrees that this is a good idea.

The single outcome of the meeting is another meeting.

Each character communicates differently, and there's a motivation behind each style:

> **Claudia's** objective in hosting the meeting is pure reassurance. Pup Sup is their newest and largest client, and she wants to make sure that they're happy. But as the senior person in the room, she doesn't want to be accused of putting all her eggs in one basket with the shiny new client. That's why she hired the external consultant, Chen.

> **Caroline** is completely unprepared for this meeting. The main thought she has running through her head is 'Please don't ask any questions. Please don't ask any questions. Please don't ask any questions.' It's not Caroline's

fault she feels this way. She's working on twelve different client accounts currently. Why does she have so many? Because Caroline is really good at her job. If Caroline had to attend fewer meetings, she might have more time to do some actual work. She doesn't have time do a summary, so she avoids agreeing to one. She tells herself that she'll have a handle on things by next week, but she won't. She'll be too busy rehearsing the next pitch.

Tom and Sven aren't involved in this project intensively yet. But they're both gunning for a promotion. The way they're going to do this is to talk over each other, shoot down ideas and throw up problems (that aren't really problems), which they can then heroically step in and solve.

Eva is the most junior member of the team and is closest to the client. She is desperate to say something, but every time she thinks about inputting with a project update, something in her head tells her that what she's about to say won't be good enough. She assumes that after the meeting is over, a secret meeting will be held without her, in which they all discuss how her silence is a clear sign of her professional incompetence.

Chen knows what day rate her company is charging Pop & Cork and feels as though she desperately needs to justify it at every possible opportunity.

Greg believes that the meeting is going well. He's pleased that this is a job that doesn't require much actual work. So far, it's mostly been meetings. Greg is good at meetings.

The client is excited for the project to start.

There's a lot going on under the surface of meetings. But think of how this whole scene might have unfolded had there been no undercurrent of ego. Imagine if the objective of the meeting had simply been announced at the start and then with a careful eye on the clock, various voices had contributed until the objective had either been fully met or they'd come as close as possible in the time set aside. What a world that would be.

Let's have a look at some different roles and how to play them.

The Host

Before anything else, the first thing to do as the host is to establish whether or not a meeting is necessary. This will ensure you avoid the most common mistake – holding a meeting that doesn't have a clear objective.

Start with the end goal and then work backwards. In an ideal world, what are you looking to achieve? What is the best format for that outcome? If the answer is a meeting (as opposed to an email, call or one-on-one conversation), make a list of all the best-placed people to help reach that outcome. This is your meeting, so it's your responsibility to ensure that it's a productive use of time for all the participants.

Leaders of conglomerates have all identified that effective, efficient meetings drive their business forward, and meetings that are a waste of time are, well, a waste of time. Many of them have come up with unusual but ingenious ways of tackling the problem. Elon Musk, for example, has enforced an internal policy that states that anyone who finds themselves in a meeting in which they feel they no longer have anything to contribute is encouraged to get up and walk out, without the others so much as raising an eyebrow. Jeff Bezos has determined that the most successful meetings are ones that don't contain too many contributors, leading to what he calls the 'Two Pizza' rule. A single meeting should never contain more people than the amount that two pizzas could feed.

These somewhat unorthodox rules might not work for every situation, so instead consider the more conventional (but often unfollowed) advice from Mary Barra, ex-CEO of General Motors. She strongly believed that meetings should be about having conversations. It's deeply frustrating when people use meeting time to present information that could have been circulated as a pre-read beforehand, which would instead have maximised discussion and minimised sharing information.

Among my clients, a chief operating officer realised how much money was being wasted on employees spending time in meetings after receiving an invitation to one that the host indicated 'shouldn't take longer than four hours'. She took the innovative approach of employing a consultant to attend meetings internally and track wasted time in terms of money. The consultant calculated the total sum by adding up the salaries of the attendees for every minute where nothing was happening. For example, if the group deviated from the objective of the meeting for as little as five minutes, this would cost five minutes' worth of the combined salaries of each person sitting around that table. In a room of eight senior managers, even a small amount of time wasted would rack up quite an alarming bill, the total of which would be announced at the end of the meeting. In just a few months she had minimised lateness, decreased the number of participants in the room and reduced the length of most meetings to under forty minutes.

So before scheduling anything, ask yourself, does this need to be a face-to-face meeting? Or could it be a phone call? Or even just an email with a deadline? And as with all advice in this book, take a big step back and ask yourself, what is the one purpose of having this conversation? What is the reason this needs to happen here, now, and with this particular group of people?

If it turns out that the meeting is necessary, then here's how to make it an as effective use of the everyone's time as possible:

Stick to the objective

To be a good meeting host requires one thing: a clear objective that is set and stuck to. That's it. Clarify that objective in the invite, at the start of the meeting and throughout. Be honest in your expression of the objective and state the motivation behind it: 'I'm looking for a project update on Cham-paw because I really want this client to be impressed by us. The objective of this meeting is that we all feel reassured we're going in the right direction.'

Then throughout the meeting keep the attendees focused on moving towards that agreed outcome. If you feel it's going off topic, steer it back with a simple 'I'm conscious of time here, so let's get back to . . .' or 'That's a really valid point, so let's come back to it another time. For now, we've got to focus on . . .'

Set ground rules

This is your meeting, so set ground rules at the start. That includes length of meeting, the tone (open, structured, informal, etc.) and basics including cameras off/on, and laptops, phone on the desk or out of sight.

Paraphrase and summarise

Be brave enough to step in throughout and paraphrase lengthy points or clarify ones that seem muddled. If a speaker has said something in a convoluted way, find the core of their message by paraphrasing it back to them. For example, 'So you're saying the client has to move from their current branding to something different to attract new customers?' Then wait for them to confirm. If a speaker makes a point that you are struggling to understand, then the chances are you're not the only one around the table who feels that way. Encourage them to be clearer by saying, 'Can you clarify that for me, please?' And keep going until everyone in the room comprehends it.

At the end, you'll need to summarise to ensure that everyone has the same understanding of what's been discussed. It's amazing how often meetings happen where people have taken away totally different meanings of what's been said.

Your final job is to summarise briefly everything that's happened, agree on an action plan and confirm who's doing what before they walk away from the meeting.

Make space

Don't let Sven and Tom dominate when it's Eva who actually has relevant information. You don't want to shoot them down, but you do want to make space for Eva's voice. Try 'I just want to jump in here and get Eva's opinion on that. I know she's been the last person here to have spoken to the client. Do you have anything to add, Eva?'

'Making space' includes you. If you find you do the minority of the speaking but the majority of the guidance, then that's a very good sign. Don't be that dick who calls a meeting just so that other people can listen to your voice.

The Attendee

As an attendee to a meeting, your main objective is to contribute, regardless of whatever invisible lines you may have drawn up in your head around hierarchy and social structure. Don't be afraid to say what you want to say even if it doesn't go along with what the majority is saying. In fact, you should express your opinion *especially* if it doesn't go along with what the rest of the group is saying. Groupthink is a psychological concept introduced by Irving Janis in 1972 after studying a variety of key historical events where the group consensus resulted in a very poor decision being made and causing chaos – the Bay of Pigs invasion being a classic example. Janis noticed that a group of humans, in their relentless desire for consensus, would often simply go along with the opinions of the majority, overriding critical thinking and stifling open dialogue.

This theory may in part explain the collapse of Kodak. Once a giant of the photography industry, when in 1975 it was pitched a digital camera prototype by one of its own engineers, the leadership team decided over a series of meetings to dismiss the new technology, fearing it would destroy their business. Dissenting voices were ignored or marginalised, and the prevailing mindset was to protect the film business at all costs as opposed to embracing the new technology, which would have allowed the company to stay at the forefront of the industry.

Adjust your mindset. It's not just the voices at the top that matter. A meeting is not a binary test of your ideas or contributions. In fact, they're usually not about you at all, which is a relief. But you and your ideas have value. This is evidenced in the fact that you've been invited along. Yes, there are louder voices in the room, but volume does not indicate importance. Take this pressure off yourself to say the 'right' thing and stop imagining that everything that comes out of your mouth has to be mind-blowingly impressive.

Allow yourself to be average. Your contribution to the meeting doesn't have to be a ten out of ten. Aim for a six or seven. If there's nothing you want to say, then don't say anything. But listen, nod along and make notes, then when there is something to say, say it. Don't feel as if you need to say it perfectly either. 'Ums' and 'errs' are just a natural part of speaking and show that you're trying to verbalise a thought. Just get the message out.

Imagine if your role at the meeting was not to speak but to turn up and hand out slices of delicious cake to hungry attendees. Imagine how loved and applauded you'd be. Even the people who didn't want a slice of cake would still appreciate your thoughtfulness. Does your verbal contribution to the meeting have a lower value than a wedge of sponge cake? No, of course not. Your input is far higher, and it's about time you treated it as such.

Here's how to ensure your voice is heard:

Prepare your points

Firstly, the moment the event lands in your inbox, you should ensure you know why you've been invited and what the objective of the meeting is. Ask for clarification before you attend if it isn't immediately obvious. Once you have a clear understanding of the goal of the meeting, consider how your contributions can help the group come closer to that pre-agreed outcome. Ask yourself, if you were limited to making no more than three points in this conversation, what would you want them to be? This will help you define and prioritise the messages you'd like to land. If you have a feeling that your suggestions might be challenged, imagine the sort of challenge you might receive, and prepare to counteract it.

Deliver your points

While being careful not to talk over anyone else's idea, find (or make) space for your message to land. Ask questions if they'll help other attendees expand their thinking.

If you're nervous about interjecting, you can start small. Expose yourself to the fear of speaking up by beginning with a few micro-contributions. These can be nods, eye contact, smiles or the occasional 'OK' or 'Uh-huh'. Then build up to short statements to agree or to clarify, such as 'That's a good idea' or 'Can you expand on that?' or 'What do we want that to look like?' Set yourself a series of short tasks such as these to complete, building up your comfort level until you're sharing full ideas and statements with the group.

Then, when the time comes, just f**king say it. And whether what you've said is met with silence, applause or indifference, don't bother spending any time overanalysing it or tearing yourself apart because you think you could've said it so much better. Instead, stay tuned into the conversation as it moves around the table rather than getting caught up in your own thoughts.

Remember, you're here to meet that initial objective that was set out at the start, and there isn't time for a deep dive into your own insecurities. By focusing on the ultimate objective of the meeting and not your own headspace, you'll not only be a more effective contributor, but you'll feel a huge amount of relief as you pivot from inwards to outwards. It takes time and practice to make this your automatic reaction post-statement, but it is well worth doing, because you'll master the art of caring less and saying more.

For bonus points, link back to other people's ideas and add your own perspective to them. For example: 'I want to come back to what Chen was saying there about the change in direction. I think it would be good to . . .'

Congratulations. You have now been a key participant in an effective meeting.

Online Meetings

Post-Covid it became apparent that even the wealthiest companies around the world no longer needed to fly their top executives from Sydney to New York City for a thirty-minute presentation. What it also meant was that all of us needed to embrace technology that could, on occasion, be unpredictable. Once, during the height of the pandemic, when I had just over a hundred prospective clients on a Zoom call, the internet simply dropped out mid-sentence. While I was frantically banging the WiFi box on the floor, a neighbour popped their head around the door and, red-faced, informed me that their bored five-year-old had been pulling random cables out in our shared corridor and that it was possible that my internet cable had been one of them. After the child had been apprehended, I returned to the Zoom call to find all one hundred faces waiting patiently for me to come back and finish my talk. To me, the debacle had felt as though it lasted about half an hour; in reality, only five or six minutes had passed. Rule number one – technology can and will go wrong. It is out of your control and panicking does not help.

The other big rule in online meetings is that everything should be shorter and sharper than it would be in real life. Screens are going to drain people a lot faster, so accommodate smaller-than-usual attention spans by making sure everything is delivered as a high-level overview, wherever possible. Not only will a more concise approach ensure a more productive meeting, but you'll also be demonstrating respect for other people's time – the most valuable commodity they have. Normally, if someone took your most precious possession from right under your nose, there's a chance they'd go to prison. Bear that in mind before you send an invite for a Monday morning four-hour Teams meeting. No one should be monologuing for longer than fifteen minutes, after which you should interact with the audience. It could be as simple as a hands-up/hands-down poll, a group activity or even a break.

What then of Pop & Cork? After various communication workshops, they will start to focus less on their own internal monologues and more on the objectives of the meetings they attend. Claudia and Caroline will relax with time and learn to trust themselves – their discomfort comes from one very positive place, which is that they are both excellent at what they do.

After a few honest conversations, Caroline will know who in her team she can confidently outsource work to, which will take the pressure off her and reassure Tom and Sven that their careers are going in the right direction. Eva will learn that her voice matters just as much as the rest of the team.

And I'm not a gambling woman, but I reckon after some steep learning curves, there's no reason why Greg shouldn't end up running the place.

8

A CREATIVE CONVERSATION

We're running out of ideas.

That's because fresh or even good ideas are incredibly hard to generate, and we very rarely give ourselves the time or the space required to come up with them. But if you need to develop a piece of communication that'll blow your competitors out of the water, you're going to have to step outside your office once in a while.

That's exactly what happened in 1967, when Heinz, an American food-processing company, was facing a problem. It needed to come up with a slogan that proved to its UK consumers that its tins of baked beans should be their one and only option, which was hard to do back in a time when Britain was a nation fuelled almost exclusively by canned goods.

Maurice Drake is the writer credited for devising the slogan 'Beanz Meanz Heinz', the line that metaphorically and physically knocked its competitors off the shelves. His team had been playing around to find a message that would work for a month or so, when Drake decided to do something different.

'We were a bit stuck, so, as I was the head of the group, I took the team down to The Victoria, behind the agency in Mornington Crescent, where we sat around with beer and sandwiches.'

It was here that inspiration struck. Not in an agency meeting room, or behind a screen, but down at The Victoria, with a notepad and a pen.

If you go into a UK supermarket today, this product is often the only baked-bean option available. Three words were enough to put Heinz Baked Beanz so far ahead of its competitors that it feels as though they've almost given up.

In 1994, four directors at Pixar had a different problem. *Toy Story* had been a monumental success, and now the pressure was on them to develop another brilliant idea. So what did they do? They left the office and went to get something to eat. Using this long-forgotten art of sacking it off and going for lunch, they came up with the ideas for *A Bug's Life*, *Monsters, Inc.*, *Finding Nemo* and *WALL-E*, films collectively now worth well over $2 billion. Using ideas sketched on paper napkins, they bounced off each other until they'd fleshed out new characters, stories and worlds during what is now famously known as 'The Billion Dollar Lunch'. Hidden City Café, the host of one of the world's most valuable conversations, can actually be seen in the background of *Monsters, Inc.*, as testimony to its inspirational power.

The connecting factor here is that both conversations took place guiltlessly and wholeheartedly, away from desks, which is exactly why when I suggest to clients that we could go for a walk outside their office, you can almost see the blood drain from their faces. They see it as skiving. A walk should be reserved for the weekend. Something personal, done with your closest family members. Something to accommodate the mental wellbeing of the dog. To leave the office in working hours should be reserved for fantasy films and fictional characters like Ferris Bueller. If you need to generate an idea, they think, that's exactly what the ideas room is for. I have encountered these rooms before. They're often covered in AstroTurf, littered in beanbags or, on one occasion, a dusty ball pit. A place in which ideas are expected to be punched out like a snack from a vending machine. They became popular in the early 2000s and have now become as inspiring as the person who reminds the more creative thinkers in a team that 'our client's budgetary restraints just won't make that a feasible option'.

At the edge of the City, plenty of these rooms still exist, although there certainly aren't any in the office of one of my favourite clients – the chief investment officer of an enormous asset management fund. If I were to take you to Liverpool Street station and ask you to pick out an individual who you thought might be in charge of billions and billions of investors' money, Philip would probably be the last person you'd pick. Wily and disarmingly honest, he had a razor-sharp sense of humour and a Glaswegian accent, which, much like all carriers of a dangerous weapon, he would use only when it was absolutely, totally essential that he should. He insisted that all sessions were held on walks where he could get away from his glass tower of a workplace, before he presented his latest challenge to me, with one hand wrapped around a black coffee and the other ready to point at invisible board members.

During one particular walk, he described his current dilemma, which had generated a lot of media interest that he'd have to address at an upcoming press conference. Our method was to head off on a walk together and dissect each issue while allowing the conversation to deviate, prompted by whatever distraction popped up. This was easy to do when we were constantly exposed to the external stimulus of East London, in the heart of the financial district. I would ask him astoundingly naive questions about how asset management worked, and he would ask me who Rita Ora was and why she was being used to sell Coca-Cola. Not all our questions had clear answers. On one occasion, we came across The Broadgate Venus, a 5-tonne sculpture of a voluptuous nude lady reclining the sunshine that pours into Exchange Square. 'I hadn't realised they'd gone ahead with that piece I've so obviously been the inspiration for,' he mused. I laughed and asked him what he thought the meaning behind the art was. 'In this location? A warning against greed perhaps.'

'She doesn't look like greed has been her downfall' I replied. 'I'd say she looks pretty happy about things.'

'Well, she's been here since the eighties. Back then, it was good to be greedy.'

Weeks later, the conference took place, and I was informed that the highlight of the afternoon was Philip energetically demanding that everyone assembled in the room go down into the square to look at the enormous Venus, a visual metaphor for the changing attitudes of investors. While it was unclear whether any of them actually went, the articles that came out of the conference reflected an understanding of his key message: now was not the time for risky strategies. 'I don't know where the hell he gets his ideas from,' said the messenger.

As you go through this book, you may be alarmed at just how often it requires you to come up with something from nothing. As we grow more and more addicted to a handheld screen that reads our brains and provide us with something we're guaranteed to find entertaining, we're losing that touch of madness that often ignites a fire.

How do you come up with something brilliant? How do you have conversations that spark new solutions or fresh material out of old ideas? And once you've come up with something, how do you keep it going? Here is how you force yourself back into the 1990s, when creative conversations had to take place daily because LinkedIn didn't yet exist, and no one was posting their top ten tips on being #curious or #playful.

Think of a favourite funny film, cartoon, TV series or stand-up artist. As casually as the comedy comes, a simple joke can be the result of a highly complex process, *Saturday Night Live* being an excellent example of this. If you're not familiar with the concept of the show, on Monday ideas for sketches are pitched, on Tuesday the scripts are written, on Wednesday the sketches are read by the cast members and selected for airing, then on Friday and Saturday they frantically rehearse up until the final performance, which happens in front of a live audience. When writers or comedians are under pressure to create something from nothing, they use a framework to encourage them to bounce ideas around and find something that develops into a humorous situation. We're going to use some of those principles here to turn a predictable conversation into a plethora of dynamic ideas.

Rule 1: Find a new environment

Anywhere will do, as long as you leave your screens behind. Google fact-checking can come later. For now, you just have to keep going with whatever you've got – even the loosest threads of some vague creative suggestions. Remember the days when you used to go to a pub and your mate who always embellished stories would say with perfect confidence the most ridiculous things? That mate is much easier to prove wrong now that they can easily be shot down with a quick search around on the internet. It's a much more accurate conversation now, but a lot less entertaining.

Rule 2: Take out 'No', bring in 'Yes, and . . .'

This is one of the basic rules of improv comedy sessions, and it's used to reject all restrictions for the moment. It's all too easy to get wrapped up in practicalities or deny an idea. Phrases such as 'We don't have enough time to do that'; 'That's physically impossible'; 'That's just not who we are/I am' may well be correct, but they're going to deny the powerfully impossible suggestions from happening. Tina Fey, who worked as a head writer on *Saturday Night Live*, gives an excellent example of this in her book *Bossypants*:

So if we're improvising and I say, 'Freeze, I have a gun', and you say, 'That's not a gun. It's your finger. You're pointing your finger at me', our improvised scene has ground to a halt. But if I say, 'Freeze, I have a gun!' and you say, 'The gun I gave you for Christmas! You bastard!' then we have started a scene because we have AGREED that my finger is in fact a Christmas gun.

Back in the corporate world, the same person who helpfully reminds a person with an idea that their idea is completely out of touch with reality does that same thing as the person who brings reality into the scene. It would have had the same effect if anyone had reminded the Pixar directors that ants can't talk and monsters aren't real. Instead, agree for a moment that there are no practical boundaries and, just briefly, you're just going to see where you get to by playing with a blank cheque. The word 'No' should, for a set amount of time, be off the table.

What should be encouraged are the words 'Yes, and . . .' Perfect for when one creative throws something completely outrageous into the room, and another person jumps on it with something even wilder. Once you've finished your moment of madness, then you can bring in those pesky practicalities. But see if you can reconcile the two. Is there a way you can make the outlandish idea work, but on a smaller budget?

Rule 3: Make statements

Perfectionists will struggle here, but pretend for a moment that there are no standards. Imagine a meeting in which you can say anything that you think is helpful to the situation, regardless of whether it is 'good' or not. One of the greatest blockers that exists in the corporate world is that many professionals engage in silent competitions over who can say the 'best' thing. The result of this is rarely a room full of phenomenal content but a room with two people in a game of one-upmanship, while the others would rather say nothing at all than something that they feel doesn't meet the invisible standards that have been put in place. If you care less about how other people will react to your statement, then the freer you'll feel about just f**king saying it. Let go. Tell yourself that today you have full permission to be average. The relief! The joy! The creativity! The failure! F**k it!

Rule 4: Make other people look good

This framework for cutting loose can be incredibly freeing, but your new-found audacity comes with a warning label. If you indulge in your new bombastic attitude too much, you can inadvertently come across as, well, a bit of a dick. But you also don't want to shut down your recklessness for fear of treading on anyone's toes. How do you find a balance? Easy. You bring others along with you. It doesn't matter if the other party is more cynical or calmer, as long as they don't shut you down. In fact, that's the basis of some of the great comedy duos. If you're working on your own with this, why not bring another party in, ask them just to 'go with it' for a bit and see what they come up with.

In a group, this is fundamental. Be the leader who says very little other than the occasional 'Keep going with that', or 'Tell me more', and you'll suddenly find you have a roomful of people who aren't afraid of saying the 'right' or 'wrong' thing any more. The result might be slightly unhinged, but it'll certainly be different, and that alone is worth the risk. You have to allow people to go fully out before you rein them (gently) back in, and that won't happen unless they feel they've been given full carte blanche. Remember, no one will look silly if everyone looks silly.

Rule 5: Care less

I was going call this bit 'finding your authentic self' but, to be honest, that phrase has become so hackneyed that you know whenever someone uses it, they're being the opposite of their authentic self. If you want to know what it truly means to care less, then look to the masters of misrule: Miriam Margolyes, Rik Mayall (along with most of the characters he played) and even Billy Mack from *Love Actually* (played by the brilliant Bill Nighy). What do all of them have in common? They behave as though they have nothing to lose. Miriam Margolyes on Graham Norton's chat show is always the most entertaining guest. She openly admits she's never heard of whichever A-list celebrity she's found herself next to and always tells the most outrageous stories. Every time she's asked on, she behaves in a way that suggests she won't be invited back, which probably explains why she's now appeared on it a total of eleven times. Find a way of being naughty without being disrespectful and you'll stand with the greats. See the rules, work around them, and you'll create astronomical change. Just like the person who refuses to use slides for a five-minute presentation. Or the person who says, 'The shit has hit the fan', when the shit hits the fan.

Or the person who bravely, boldly asks the event managers if each speaker needs to fill a forty-five-minute slot when ten minutes would be ample. Build on these tiny acts of rebellion every day, and you'll become unstoppable.

One last thing. If ever you find yourself near Liverpool Street, go and look at the 5-tonne Venus. Marvel, too, at the city workers bustling past her as if not once in their lives have they ever, or will they ever, notice her glorious presence. The big secret in becoming more creative is to look up, around and out. Even if it's just for five minutes a day, put your screen down and look at the complete lunacy around you – the inspiration for the next great idea might be right in front of your face.

9

SELF-PROMOTION WITHOUT FEELING NAUSEOUS

Even if you can't see all of them, an audience of 10 million can be quite unsettling.

Events of this scale have the unusual effect of turning speakers into mini-celebrities, and the unfamiliar public attention can be as exciting as it is disconcerting.

It's five years ago, and I am sitting backstage with my client who is about to find herself thrust figuratively and literally into the spotlight. She has just done a phenomenal job of delivering her talk at an event that is being live-streamed across the world, and as we wait in the wings for the whole thing to come to an end, my client nudges me and holds up her phone. We gawp as an aggressive waterfall of notifications floods her screen, and she looks at me with a blend of relief and bewilderment. I did warn her this might happen, but I could tell she didn't really believe me. Twenty minutes ago, her followers were made up of fellow school mums, her cycling club and old university mates, but now everyone from a popular car journalist to a celebrity podcaster want to be her new best friend.

Months, maybe even a year of work, has gone into the planning of this event, and the production levels have felt as if they've been on scale with the coronation of any European royal. It certainly seems as though a new leader has been crowned in the corporate world, and as she steps out onto the enormous stage for one final bow, I can almost hear 'Zadok the Priest' playing. On a TV screen in the green room, I can see the angle from the back of the auditorium, revealing a view of which she is completely unaware: hundreds of smartphone screens recording her, some already uploading the footage to the internet. With this outpouring of excitement and celebration, it suddenly feels as if she is inadvertently at the centre of the universe. Yet alongside this intense feeling of potential empowerment, there's a growing sense of exposure.

A few days later, I am back at home, enjoying the steady stream of media coverage that is still flowing from the event. If she's really made it, I think to myself, she'll be turned into a meme any moment now. Just as I am having this thought, as if I have manifested her presence, her name appears on my phone. I answer the call and brace myself for the exultation to follow. Instead, she talks quickly and calmly, just as people do when there is an emergency and they have no time for emotions or chitchat. She explains that an article has emerged on the internet of which she is the target. Somewhere in New York, two competitors have clubbed together and written nothing short of a poison-pen review of her recent performance, and all the joy she was feeling has evaporated as she enters crisis mode. She forwards the article to me, and I click the link with an uncomfortable tightness growing in my throat.

This rare example of a nightmare coming true perfectly embodies the deep fear we all face when stepping into the limelight: the dread that if we dare to put ourselves out there, someone, somewhere, won't like it. Worse than that, they'll feel brave enough, among all the compliments that are being thrown at you, to be the one responsible for pointing out what you suspected all along: you don't deserve any of it. The greatest block to self-promotion is – once again – that deep-rooted care for the opinions of people you never have and never will meet.

On top of this sense of not wanting to put our head above the parapet, if you're British, there's something ingrained in your DNA that prevents you from talking too much about yourself at all, especially with regard to anything good you might have done. As a British person, everything you do and say is somehow designed to undermine yourself, which would explain why we struggle so much in interviews or pitches, whereas in diners across the USA, not saying you serve 'The World's Best Cup of Coffee' is to miss a trick. Americans have made self-promotion an artform.

Even the word 'self-promotion' seems to fill my UK-based clients with disgust. We can promote our company, our clients and our colleagues, but to showcase our own abilities seems outrageously indulgent. Obscene even. Talking about ourselves in any kind of congratulatory way fills us with a sense of loathing so strong that we're willing to sacrifice exciting opportunities because of it.

My American clients see working with me as an invaluable investment in themselves and don't think twice about signing up for any event or occasion that might elevate their profile. In contrast, my British clients will often see me in almost totally secrecy, even with a sense of shame. While there's something valuable in self-deprecation and humility, too much can result in a lack of external recognition alongside the internal struggles. There must be a way to scrape off some of that big, loud American swagger and spread it across the next opportunity to raise your profile. Keeping quiet about the great thing you have to offer might feel more comfortable, but it might result in you missing out on something huge.

Before the rise of social media, clever marketing might have been as simple as naming your business 'AAA Taxi Service' to secure the top spot in the phone book. Today, having an online presence is no longer just an option – it's essential for most businesses' survival and growth. While concerns about losing the human touch due to over-reliance on screens are certainly valid, they might also be somewhat shortsighted. Although personality, reputation and character matter now more than ever, they can absolutely be conveyed online. Yet this opportunity for mass exposure comes down to how willing you are to put yourself out there. So let's dive into exactly how to do self-promotion without nausea coming along for the ride.

Self-Promotion Without the Self-indulgence

In London, one business consultant I worked with employed me because he'd seen the short videos I endlessly publish across social media. After speaking to me about how effective this tactic was in attracting new clients, he wanted in. We found a sunny street in East London, we brought filming equipment and microphones, we crafted a punchy script, and we practised. Soon, it was time to hit the big red button. I gave him a final gesture to encourage a facial expression of any kind and leaned forward to press 'record'.

>Him: Wait.

I looked up, ready to be told the lighting wasn't right or that there was unexpected background noise.

>Him: I can't do it. It's too much. I can't be this arrogant.
>Me: I thought this was what you wanted.
>Him: I can't say that about myself.
>Me: Which bit?
>Him: The bit where I talk about myself. Where I say how good I am.
>Me: But this is a video about you. You're demonstrating to your audience how good you are at your job. And you are good at your job.
>Him: Yeah, I am good at what I do. But I can't actually say that, can I?

We had to abandon the whole recording session. All that time, money and effort lost because at the last moment, that ambition to self-promote turned into an unpalatable feeling of self-indulgence.

It took a few months before the client returned, and this time he went through with the recording. This outcome was nothing to do with my powers of persuasion, not at all connected with what I said to convince him to change his mind. Instead, a few days earlier, a competitor had published videos of their own to much acclaim. Spurred on by the idea that 'if I don't do it, then someone else will', my client finally created his own video series that helped solve client conundrums, narrated case studies and gave tips and advice to potential new customers. Self-promotional? Yes. But not self-indulgent. If what you communicate offers value, you'll always stay on the right side of the line and avoid using the audience as a tool for personal validation.

My business consultant client accepted that making videos in which he was the producer, director and star of the show was going to feel, well, uncomfortable. Yet when he started to receive messages from viewers who were genuinely delighted that he was sharing information that they found useful, that cringey feeling didn't feel quite so cringey any more.

On top of this, new business enquiries started to land in his inbox, often with the words 'I was thinking about that video you posted last week, and I was wondering if . . .' It's good to be modest, and a controllable amount of impostor syndrome is healthy, but if you're holding back on self-promotion because you can't talk about the work you do with pride instead of shame, then don't be surprised if opportunities start slipping away from you.

It's not only individuals who experience this sense of insecurity when it comes to self-promotion but businesses too – with a different output. When putting material out there publicly, they tend to hide behind statistics, such as the age, size and history of the company, instead of what the audience is there to hear about when it comes to promotion: the solutions on offer. One consultancy firm I worked with suffered from this exact issue. The team had discovered who their competitors were in a forthcoming pitch and wearily described the situation to me as 'We're the only names in the line-up we don't recognise.' Because of this self-doubt, their opening gambit was an 'about us' slide, listing all their offices around the world, detailing how many employees were sitting in each place and extensively listing the services they offered. They had decided that this was the best way to convince the other party they could (in their words) 'keep up with the big boys'. Their own insecurity sat at the heart of the delivery, and as a result, their pitch came across as an intense request for validation. In reality, their potential client already knew how they lined up in comparison to 'the big boys' and still felt they were worth adding to the beauty parade.

To reset the approach, I asked them to explain what they felt they could offer that their competitors could not. Ironically, the answer was in the one thing they were trying to hide – they weren't the biggest, or the most well known, but the flip side of that was that they could move much faster, more flexibly, and would work much harder for their client (and, of course, at a competitive price). With their perceived weakness now proudly put forward as their greatest asset, they not only felt more confident in talking about their work but could also easily identify case studies with other clients where their speed, agility and dedication had resulted in an outcome that couldn't have been guaranteed with their larger competitors. Now, with their case studies forming the introduction of the pitch, they were showcasing solutions to problems that the panel in front of them were experiencing. What they ended up delivering was exactly what their audience wanted to hear and explained in a far more assertive and compelling way. When they (unsurprisingly) made it through to the final round of pitching, the approach we took was simply to use storytelling, brainstorming all the potential issues or missed opportunities that they thought the panel might be concerned about and then matching up each of them with an example of how they'd turned that around for a previous client. It didn't feel like uncomfortable showing-off because what they were offering was not only the truth but a demonstration of their expertise in action.

If you follow the rule of 'it's not about me, it's about them', then you easily avoid your own insecurities about self-indulgence infiltrating a message that would otherwise blow your audience away. Instead, inspire your client by showing them how great *they* could become – with your help.

For example, if you say the following: *I'm really amazing. I'm the most qualified, highest-educated and most experienced person in the room, so I'm the one you should pick to work with.* Then that has an egotistical edge. There's no space for the client either. And, frankly, it's a bit bland.

But if you take a different approach, such as this story-led example: *I want to tell you a story about how last week I helped my client achieve something they didn't even think was possible, and I'm going to show you how you can do the same* . . . Then you get all the self-promotion you need without that nauseating feeling.

And it's way more interesting too.

The same might be true of a personal trainer trying to recruit new customers. They could either stand in the street handing out fliers that list their various qualifications and sporting achievements, or they simply hand out a photo of one flabby, headless torso labelled: 'BEFORE', contrasted to a less flabby torso labelled 'AFTER' coupled with the caption: *This is what Steve R. from Bedford looks like after just six short personal-training sessions!* Time and time again, the headless torso wins out because the focus is on the audience.

How to Create Your Personal Elevator Pitch

So if you don't prove your credibility with lists of qualifications, awards or achievements, how do you create a convincing statement that instantly explains what it is that you do on a daily basis? If you want to pin a post to the top of your Instagram squares or LinkedIn profile with an immediate encapsulation of what it is you offer, what exactly should it say?

The 'elevator pitch' is a useful hypothetical exercise that encourages professionals to come up with a way of introducing and promoting themselves in a less than a couple of minutes. These days, I'd argue you have significantly less time than an elevator ride, especially when it comes to self-promotion on social media, and the shorter the statement the better. To come up with your own version, continue to follow that golden rule of 'It's not about you. It's about your audience.' You want to explain immediately how what you're offering is helpful.

For example, look at the role of someone who works in cyber security. A typical introduction might look like this: *I'm a cyber-security analyst. I specialise in securing systems against cyber-attacks and malware by fortifying systems against a wide range of digital threats.*

Yet this isn't likely to endear you to anyone outside your industry, especially not potential new clients. Instead, you'll need to come back to using a problem–solution formula to describe what you do for others: *My company sleeps safe at night knowing that while our computer systems could be attacked at any moment, I'm protecting all of it from any kind of threat.*

You'd be amazed at how often the audience benefit isn't added on. For example, if I want to quickly explain to anyone what I do, I say, 'I'm a public-speaking coach. I help my clients look good, feel confident, and sound incredible when they speak to an audience.' Then to explain my offering, I'd add something as simple: 'I take my clients from a blank piece of paper right up to the moment they step up onto the stage.'

In order to come up with your own version, ask yourself a few questions:

1. What do I do?
2. How am I helpful? What problem do I solve or what opportunity do I offer?
3. What is the positive outcome of my product/service/offering?

Write a few lines and when you think you have something that works, try it out on a few people who are external to your industry. If they immediately see the benefit of what you do, then you've found something that works and, if not, keep playing around until you find it, then reduce it down to the shortest possible statement.

Every time you're hit with the question, 'What do you do?', you can respond with an answer that instantly makes the most of the opportunity that's landed in front of you. On top of that, committing these lines to heart will instil in you an 'audience first' ethos. For podcasts, social media content, interviews and short biographies, you can reuse these lines time and time again as a springboard into storytelling. Eventually, showcasing your work through examples of what you've done for clients will become second nature, and you'll be self-promoting at every opportunity without feeling as though you have to reach for the sick bucket.

Nevertheless, on very rare occasions, there will be someone who looks at what you're doing and decides they don't like it. While it's absolutely OK for someone to disagree with you, unfounded personal criticism is more likely to come from the critic's own jealousy rather than a genuine desire to educate or offer challenge. This is known as 'cutting down the tallest poppy'. Your attackers may wish to eliminate your achievements by pointing out perceived 'errors' and enjoy being seen openly thwarting your ambition. It is easier for them to take this approach rather than try to compete with you.

This was exactly what had happened with my client who was trying to navigate her new-found fame. She had carefully ignored all the praise, dismissed all the celebration, and on some far corner of the internet, she'd found an article that was a well-written, obvious attack from two men who were outraged that she'd been given such a platform, and they hadn't. This had then been reposted on various sites by the co-writer of the article, and, in total, had accumulated around ten likes, and a couple of commendatory comments (which on deeper investigation were revealed to be from the authors themselves). Yet it felt to my client that, at last, someone had seen through it all, and that these two voices of criticism were both valid and reasonable. Once I'd finished reading the article, I asked if she felt that focusing on the angry voice of someone with an obvious motive was fair. The client agreed that listening to the feedback of someone from whom she would never seek advice was illogical.

Nevertheless, the event and the subsequent attack had left her feeling as if she was headline news, and that the whole world was now watching her every move. In reality, what seemed like a very big moment to her had not even entered into the peripherals of the majority of folk walking down the street. Both lavish praise and unfounded criticism can drain away just as quickly as they arrive: neither of them should hold undue influence over your self-perception. Ground yourself, and listen only to the voices that understand you, support you and are willing to speak directly to you.

I told my client that she was f**king brilliant.

10

A NETWORKING EVENT

I watch my client sketch out a meticulously detailed diagram of the street where his office is.

Some months before, I had been to a meeting in the same building in Manchester that he was drawing, but I hadn't been back since. The meeting took place in an enormous room with far more space than was needed for just a manager, two people from HR and me. We were all there to talk about a high-performing employee. It had been decided (by everyone except the employee) that he would benefit from working with a speech coach.

His manager, a senior leader within the company, carefully described what Ben was, what Ben was not, and what Ben should be. 'In many ways, he's our greatest asset,' she said, 'but he's also extremely difficult to deal with. He's the brain of this organisation, and without him, we'd – well, frankly, we wouldn't have a product.' She was skirting round whatever it is that she wanted to say, and I was trying to come up with a question that would make her use adjectives that meant something.

Fortunately, one of the women from HR happily dived into 'the problem'. 'What Jane is saying is that he may be a genius, but the issue is that we can't put him in front of anyone. He struggles with networking. If we could just maximise his interactions, he could run this place but, he just won't, er, talk. To anyone.' The other HR person gave his input. 'Exactly. And what we think you could do is a bit of charm school. That's what he needs. A charisma injection.' Restrained laughter followed.

I attempted to push back by describing exactly what my job was and where my limitations were, but they insisted that I should go ahead with the sessions, and now, here we were. Through my screen I was watching my client create an elaborate technical drawing in total silence, from memory.

Normally, when a client has been 'put forward' to work with me rather than approaching me of their own volition, those first few meetings are extremely difficult. I have to spend the initial hour convincing them they haven't been sent to the headmaster's office because they've done some wrong but rather as a sign that the company values them. But if corporate speak irks me, then it completely baffles Ben. He is polite, extremely quiet and endearing. And he's insisted that all of our sessions take place online, which is why I haven't been back to his office since. It's plain he's asking me to say exactly why he's been told he has to work with me. Words such as 'expanding' or 'potential' don't seem to be helping either of us.

'For example,' I say, 'I understand that there's a networking event they'd like you to go to soon. In Madrid. The company is keen that when you're there, you feel as confident as possible about speaking to potential new clients.'

Ben considers this for a moment. Of all the clients I've ever had, he is the least bothered by an extended pause and will sit in silence for as long as it takes him to reach his next thought. 'I had assumed the SAAS conference in Madrid was in relation to network monitoring. But you're saying they want me to network with people so I can sell them our product.'

I laugh. Ben does not. Despite this, Ben has a good sense of humour. He enjoys referring to his management team as 'my robot overlords' and, on occasion, 'the people upstairs' which I initially took to be a joke until Ben explained that he is speaking literally. He works on the lower ground floor of the building, which suits him. They work on the upper floors, and will occasionally get together in their vast boardroom, on the top of the building, which must have been the one I'd sat in.

I work with Ben for only a brief period of time before admitting to the HR team that I don't think there is much benefit in continuing their *My Fair Lady*-style makeover. Progress is being made, but Ben just doesn't want to ooze gravitas. He is perfectly content being Ben. To my surprise, they fight back, because Ben has apparently been the source of a major contract during his time in Madrid, and they couldn't be happier with such an encouraging and tangible result. This comes as surprise to me too and so I make a mental note to explore this revelation in my next (and potentially) last session with Ben.

Our session begins, and Ben is avoiding any mention of Madrid. Instead, he has started by doing a bit of drawing. He explained in our first session that he finds this hobby relaxing, and it helps him think about things. Picking up the computer camera to span the room, he shows me all his vast, intricate cityscapes pinned to the walls. 'It's not dissimilar to what the infrastructure of our software looks like,' he says.

I ask him how the trip went, to which he replies, 'Hot.' But after one of his characteristically heavy pauses, he smiles. 'The people upstairs are pleased with me this week. We have a new client. A very big one.'

A few days after his return from the conference, he was in an online forum for fintech experts, when one community member, who he'd been exchanging ideas with for years, expressed an interest in a user demo, convinced that Ben's software would be a vital addition to his own company's suite of customer management tools. Ben had obligingly pointed him in the direction of his upstairs overlords who'd assumed they'd connected over beers on Castellana Boulevard. The timing had simply been coincidental – Ben hadn't even touched a single *cerveza*. He went on to explain that he found some aspects of the conference tolerable. But not the social networking part. He couldn't understand why getting a bit drunk in a sweaty bar was such a vital part of his ability to do his job, so he ignored that expectation and went back to his hotel room each night. It's the small talk that kills him. He'd rather ask someone to recall the worst moment of their childhood than ask them how their journey was.

After an extensive search, his company find a salesperson who can sell their product without even having to explain the technical side of it. And Ben becomes comfortable in taking a quality-over-quantity approach. If every year he can find a client like that one, I offer, he'd never have to see me again. Ben says nothing for a bit, then he agrees.

*

The quality-over-quantity ethos is a good way to do it, but whether you want to work on one key contact over a year, or whether you have of thousands of LinkedIn connections, or if you're somewhere in between, the uncomfortable fact is that whatever your line of work, there will probably come a point when networking in some form may become necessary, and knowing how to talk to people can make it easy.

There's that bit that everyone hates – small talk. The good news is that small talk will lead to big talk, but it's up to you to make the jump from the little pond to the ocean.

Let us imagine it is Christmas. Ahhh, cosy, whimsical Christmas. It may be dark before you've even thought about leaving your desk, but when it's cold outside and warm by the fire, who cares? There are twinkly lights all over the place, and those precious few days off to do absolutely nothing except stuff your face while wearing your comfiest sweatpants are just around the corner. And just as you break away from your inbox to check whether it's started to snow yet, that's when it lands: '2025 Christmas wrap-up! Join us to Mingle and Jingle.'

Your clients, people you used to really like only a few minutes ago, are having Christmas-themed networking drinks and, naturally, you'll be expected to attend.

Just like that, the magic of the festive season is brought to a halt faster than you can say 'warm mulled wine'. You know that you'll have to talk to people you've never met, and you know you need to make more of an impact than just going in and out unnoticed. This is where you get a big slice of business from. Plus, your boss will be going, so there really is no escape.

Tips to Get You Started

For many people, the hardest part is getting started – something about going from silence to conversation seems affronting. Here's what you need to do before you even open your mouth:

1. Take a friend

If you can convince your favourite co-worker that they should also go along, then you'll increase your odds of enjoying the night, because you'll always have someone to come back to. It goes without saying that if you then spend the whole night talking exclusively to each other, you'll have missed the point of the exercise, but if the two of you have good rapport that you're happy to bring other people in to, then that's a great way of cutting through small talk and getting straight to the good stuff.

2. Smile

Walking into a room of people you barely know can seem daunting, but just think how it feels to be on the other side of that. The room itself may already be full of people desperate to have a conversation. Yes, you might feel like a bit of a fool entering a room gurning, with or without a garish Christmas jumper on, but what will happen almost immediately is that someone will start talking to you. Why? Because for a reason they can't quite put their finger on, you look like the friendliest person in the room. If holding a smile gets a little tiring, at least go in with an open mouth. Lips closed tightly together might feel natural, but a face like a clock stuck at twenty to four indicates a lack of approachability.

3. Go for groups

Your natural tendency might be to approach that one person standing on their own, but if you approach an individual, it's hard to break away from that conversation without feeling rude. Two people might be having a private conversation, so attempt to approach groups with at least three people in them. In approaching an individual, you'll feel safe because you can start a conversation from scratch, but the group will already be in mid-flow: you're already through the awkward start.

Tips to Get You Talking

Now you'll need to start talking to people. Fortunately, that is very much the expectation of the event by all participants, so throw off any ideas that just walking up to someone and starting to chat to them is 'weird'. Their attendance at the event is consent that they have agreed to talk and be talked to, even if it doesn't feel like a true reflection of how conversations start in real life.

HOW TO DO . . .

1. 'Bridget Jones' any introductions

You already know how to introduce yourself in a couple of short lines using your short elevator pitch from the chapter on self-promotion. But how do you introduce other people? There is a scene in the first Bridget Jones film, where her great pal 'Shazza' gives her a helpful networking tip ahead of a book launch that Bridget is required to attend: 'Introduce people with thoughtful details.' This is a surprisingly useful tip from the same character who inadvertently goes on to get Bridget arrested for drug smuggling in the second film. These small clues will help get the conversation off to a good start, so add them in early on. To give you the example that Mark Darcy uses: 'Ahh Natasha . . . This is Bridget Jones. Bridget works in publishing and used to play naked in my paddling pool.' Maybe don't lead with this *exact* example, even if it does happen to be true . . .

2. Compliment or make an observation

When you first meet someone, if there's anything you can say that avoids the inevitable 'Had you far to come?', then you'll be off to a much better start. 'Wow, that reindeer jumper is amazing' might prompt the other person to give you an insight into where they're from or why they chose something so gaudy and, if not, you can always ask those questions yourself. What you've done here is made the other person feel as though you've just handed them a £50 note. That's exactly what a Japanese neuroscientist called Norihiro Sadato discovered in an MRI study in 2012. It showed that when people received a genuine compliment, it activated the same part of the brain as getting a financial reward. Compliments triggered the brain's reward system, making people more likely to engage socially afterwards. The next time you needlessly worry about having nothing to offer, consider that you're walking in with a pocket full of cash to distribute. A carefully considered piece of praise goes a long way.

3. Tweaking the basics

Making small changes to typical questions might get a better result than the question the other person is fully expecting. It's fair to say that predictable questions result in predictable answers. For example, going from 'What do you do?' to 'So what have you been up to this week?' widens the question and therefore widens the answer.

Tips to Cut Through the Small Talk

I have noticed that dads all over the world have one burning question that they must ask any person visiting them: 'Which roads did you take to get here?' It's not a terrible start, but it tends to shut down things quite quickly. How do you turn small talk into big talk? Start by trusting that the other person is just as keen as you are that the conversation turns to the bit where you get to know each other – once you've covered the M4 vs the A40, of course.

The golden rule in making conversation is to worry less about how interesting you are and, instead, be interested in the other person. The more valued you can make them through question asking, the more they'll walk away from that conversation feeling as if you've made a genuine connection with each other. We've all had the experience of having someone take a genuine interest in you and interview you as though you're going on the cover of *Rolling Stone* magazine. It makes you feel like a rock star and is the verbal equivalent of a deep-tissue shoulder massage. You will find this rule in any book on networking and relationships you'll ever read, but if you're not doing it yet, then it's a message worth repeating. Asking questions is the most important rule in this chapter.

If you've never watched the reality TV show *First Dates* on Channel 4, then you're missing out. If you haven't seen the show, it's a simple premise and does exactly what it says on the tin. The viewer has a fly-on-the-wall position as an observer to a first date between two people set up by the production team. The pair have dinner together before being asked to review their date (brutally, they do this in front of the other person). The participants that do well on the show and receive positive reviews all have one thing in common – they ask questions, and then they listen intently to the answer. Those who receive lower reviews all talk about themselves breathlessly, desperate to try to prove to the other party how funny/interesting/charismatic they are, either out of (mostly) nervousness or (occasionally) arrogance. If you want a powerful lesson in self-awareness, then there is no greater resource I can point you to.

1. Follow the clues

Help the other person out. If you are thrown a typical small-talk question, offer them an answer they can explore further with you. This was easy for me to do for a period of time in my life when I lived near Baker Street. Instead of saying, 'I've come from north-west London', I'd say, 'I've come from Baker Street, very near to the Sherlock Holmes Museum.' I could almost guarantee this would result in follow-up questions. And vice versa, the moment someone drops any sort of a clue into a conversation, they are offering you something to jump on. Do not miss that opportunity to dig in.

2. Help and be helped

Practical tasks are a useful way to allow for natural interaction, especially in a first-meeting situation, where you can give the other person simple tasks to help with the hosting. They'll feel valued and it can generate further chat. For example, 'What drink would you like – hold that for me while I pour this out. I can tell you've done this before', etc., etc. Humans collaborating on a simple task, such as moving a table, instantly bond, because it leads to natural open communication followed by mutual accomplishment.

3. Reduce, reuse, recycle

So that you don't turn your series of questions into an interrogation, have some material ready. Simple, short stories and anecdotes work well, and you're more than welcome to use someone else's story if they've got a good one. If they're in the room, bring them over to tell it themselves, if you know it's something they enjoy reliving. At this point, you're practically the maestro of the orchestra.

4. Listen up

It goes without saying that you should listen. We all know that bore who jumps in on your story immediately to talk about how it relates to them, or how they had a similar experience, but somehow, theirs was somehow bigger, better or more extreme than yours. You can absolutely engage in a tennis match of story sharing, but you must avoid one-upmanship. Stay on the right side of the line by always listening in full to the other person's story, and nod or 'uh-huh' along to show engagement. In doing so you'll validate them, which fulfils their basic human need for empathy and recognition while tapping into that golden rule about making sure the other person feels valued. We have an inherent need to feel a sense of 'belonging' in a group, and the feeling of being listened to reassures us that we've built a connection. That makes life even easier for you because once a person has that sense of connection, they become far more willing to share further stories with you.

5. Vulnerability is valuable

My favourite way of building rapport in a conversation is to let the other party in on a mistake or vulnerability. This is easy for me because I seem to spill coffee on myself most mornings. If I detect a new client is a little nervous about the situation, I will point out the coffee spill and apologetically make a joke about it. They instantly realise I am as flawed a human as they are and start to relax. It doesn't mean you need to burst into tears and talk about how your hamster died many years ago, but it does mean you can allow emotions into the conversation. I always enjoy the company of the person who immediately reveals how they're feeling about the situation they're in. Something as simple as 'I always feel worried about Christmas networking events – they make me nervous I'm going to be the only one wearing a light-up jumper' goes a long way.

6. Agony Aunt

People love offering advice, so if you're comfortable to, share a genuine conundrum you've been considering and ask for their opinion. This is a really good way to get an understanding of the different personalities in the room and guarantees a variety of interesting responses. You're both sharing a vulnerability and also inviting others to share their expertise. 'Does anyone have the perfect eggnog recipe? Mine always comes out disappointingly lumpy.'

7. Call me by my name

Customer service people are brilliant at using your name to make you feel as if they know you and they've connected with you. It's also a good way to ensure you don't immediately forget it. Just don't overdo it to a point where it becomes insincere or creepy . . .

Tips for Making an Exit

There is a mutual agreement that at some point conversations have to break apart and move on. The point of a networking event is to network, so don't feel guilty about casting the net wide and gracefully exiting and entering different groups. The most endearing way I have ever seen this happen is by observing one of those people that seems to 'work the room' effortlessly. She left a group I was part of where an entertaining conversation had been taking place, but before it had had a chance to run its course, she explained to the group with a weary sigh, 'You'll have to excuse me. I really should be doing some networking here.' This had made us feel she was enjoying the conversation that this group was offering, and it was only out of duty that she had to peel herself away. It didn't really occur to us that we were part of that task. It even left the impression that she'd made time for us because she wanted to, not out of social obligation. What a great escape!

1. Make a friend, take a friend

If you find you're stuck with one person and you both know you need to move away but can't for some reason, then take them with you. If you see a group you know that you'd like to say hello to, offer to introduce them to the group. Or if there's no one else you both know, explain that you know you have a duty to network, and ask them if there's a group that you both agree look approachable. Drink anyone?

Do not make that classic mistake of getting out of things by finishing your drink and saying, 'I have finished my drink, please excuse me while I get another.' You'll either end up having the best night of your life or the worst one, but either way you'll be limiting your networking opportunities.

2. Following up

It's easy to forget this bit, but it's essential. Social media has made it possible to track someone down the next day so that you can further develop the relationship. Just mentally note their name or ask your host the next day if you forget. A short note saying how great it was to meet them and briefly referencing something you spoke about when you met is a brilliant way to keep the ball rolling.

Do not expect overnight results. Genuine connections rarely happen instantly (and if they do, they often turn out to be artificial down the line), so expect the really strong connections to take time. Care less if people like you instantly or not.

I was once in the privileged (and unusual) position of witnessing a famous pop star meet a man who would become his wealth manager. The pop star (aged nineteen at the time) was relatively new to the game and still learning to navigate the swarms of fans that now followed him wherever he went, screaming out for his attention. The wealth manager was old school, low key, and had never not worn a tie for even a day of his (extensive) professional career. The contrast between the visual appearance of the two was astonishing, but the first physical contact they made was even more remarkable. They both went to extend a hand at the same time, but the pop star raised his in a fist, leaving it hanging mid-air, ready to be 'bumped'. The wealth manager's hand had reached the fist, and without blinking, he wrapped his palm around it and pressed it up and down a few times in a firm shake. Despite that shaky start, a few weeks later the wealth manager received an email saying he was hired. He was the one, out of all the people the pop star had been introduced to, who had most resembled what the teenager imagined a wealth manager would be like.

Contrary to belief, an awkward first impression does not define the relationship, and authenticity is appreciated more than pretending to be something you're not. Awkward moments are a small sacrifice for an honest, authentic connection. Laying on a bit of charm and attention works wonders, but when we meet someone who seems unafraid to be themselves in spite of social expectations, we can't help but enjoy their company.

11

A WEDDING SPEECH

Somewhere at the bottom of a handbag I have a dessert spoon bent into a right-angle, a souvenir of the worst wedding speech I've heard.

It was a warm day in early spring, somewhere near Dorset. You might think the spoon was some quirky wedding-gift tableware or keepsake from the magician entertainer. In fact, it was just an ordinary piece of rental cutlery, and the day it took on its new form started out as a quintessential, perfectly charming wedding. Even the spectacle of pageboys in Pepto-pink cummerbunds hadn't caused undue concern, but as the day progressed, a growing sense of unease crept in.

After two perfunctory, sugar-free speeches from the father of the bride and the groom, the world-weary MC introduced a man juggling microphone, iPhone and pint. Thrusting the pint at his newly minted sister-in-law and with an over-confident nod to grinning mates, he was off. Straight off came the first two witticisms you get if you Google 'Best Man Jokes'. The first goes as follows: 'Ladies and Gentlemen, I've read that a good speech shouldn't last longer than it will take the groom to make love tonight. Thank you for listening.' (*Sits.*) The second (filched from the wickedly unfunny 1970s publication *Playboy's Complete Book of Party Jokes*) compares marriage to a deck of cards: it starts with a heart and a diamond, and ends with a club and a spade. Delivered in quick succession, they elicited scattered grins across the tables, peals of laughter from his mates. I glanced at the bride, who had adopted a tight-lipped smile.

What followed was a montage of ex-girlfriends, stag-do anecdotes and career-ending scandals that would've made even a Tory MP blush. No bodily fluid or function was omitted. As he perilously embarked on a story with ejaculation being the dead-cert punchline, I surveyed the landscape. Of my friends sitting opposite, one had gone full ostrich, breathing into her hands, whispering, 'No. Please, no . . .' The other had picked up his dessert spoon with both hands and was squeezing it so hard his knuckles were white. On the far side of the marquee, the bride's family was stony-faced, staring at their shoes. The bride's grandmother lay slumped in her wheelchair. The torture had been going for over twenty minutes, with no end in sight. As the punchline came, the assembled guests sat in silence, except for that one table who were now falling off their chairs, puce-faced and holding each other's shoulders as if they were preparing for a rugby scrum. That was followed by a handful of sentences expressing the speaker's lukewarm feelings towards the bride, and then, finally, the agony ended, the speaker strode back to his table, ready to accept his flurry of backslaps.

My friend dropped the bent spoon onto the table and I popped it into my handbag, so I'd always be reminded of the public-speaking equivalent of watching a slow-motion car crash, powerless to do anything to prevent the devastating impact that followed.

Traditional Roles

It is no longer the status quo to have only the holy trinity of wedding speakers deliver heartfelt messages of joy. Traditional events may still call on the father of the bride, the groom and the best man to make speeches, but as weddings have evolved to become more varied, the likelihood that anyone might be called on to make a speech has increased. Some weddings don't have brides; some don't have grooms; some don't have parents. These three traditional roles can be played by anyone, no one or multiple people. I have used the three traditional speeches given at a wedding simply to structure this chapter, not to dictate the roles or the people who should play them. They represent three different perspectives of one couple, regardless of who is actually involved.

The best speeches I see in this category come from a speaker who simply has something they want to say, and so they stand up and f**king say it – embodying the true spirit of 'care less'. They have a couple of sincere thank-yous to make, a funny story to tell and a sentimental statement. Someone speaking because they *want* to say something can often feel more authentic than those who must speak out of convention. I have seen a mother of the bride speak because she found a letter the bride had written to the groom when they were children. I have seen a bride speak because she plainly wanted to tell the (very funny) story of how she met her groom and their recovery from a devastating first impression. And I personally have delivered more than a few bridesmaid speeches (because if you knew a baker, you'd get them to do the cake, right?). I have seen a same-sex wedding where tradition was blended brilliantly with something more alternative, resulting in six fantastic mini-speeches throughout the day. Family, friends, godparents, even children are welcome to play the roles I have set out below.

Regardless of who you are and what your role is, the main rule still applies: don't go on for too long.

The Basics

There is a wedding speech scale. To understand what it looks like, there are two film scenes that accurately reflect both ends of the spectrum.

One is beautifully demonstrated in the 2013 film *I Give It a Year*. Stephen Merchant (playing best man to the lead), delivers a train wreck, opening with, 'For-ni-cation – excuse me – for an *occasion*, like this one . . .' There's a total lack of self-awareness combined with the mindless enthusiasm of a golden retriever. He stumbles through a monologue as bland as it is offensive, creating the funniest scene in the film by far. The naivety should make you feel sorry for the character, but the thoughtlessness of his delivery – 'Rachel, love [the bride], you're a solid eight out of ten' – means that you're left squirming. This is a big, fat zero.

If you're after a ten, look no further than the ultimate wedding of the 1990s. Hugh Grant as 'Charles' not only set alight the hearts of Sloane Rangers across the world but also set a terrifying new precedent for best men speeches to be not just funny, but thoughtful. After *Four Weddings*, they had to be good, noticeably good. The speech Grant's character delivers is self-deprecating, warm, full of irony. And brief. This is a ten.

But how do you stay on the upper side of that scale? How do you make an audience laugh in recognition, not out of embarrassment? Being asked to deliver a wedding speech is both the ultimate compliment and a great curse, so if you're feeling mixed emotions, there's good reason for that. I've had many clients who feel relatively confident giving speeches at work and so are confused when they're unexpectedly nervous about speaking in front of wedding guests.

Why does delivering a disappointing sales update to the CEO seem achievable, but talking to a hundred people you know seems impossible? The answer is obvious: it's because you care. While the ethos of this book is to 'care less', under these circumstances, it doesn't mean you care less about the people you're speaking about, but it does mean you should care less about how you will be perceived by the audience outside that specific group. You rightly care far more about not letting your best friend or your daughter down than you care about a numbers meeting. That's why you're putting so much pressure on yourself for this to be the best speech you've ever given. The problem with setting the bar that high is that it leads to huge levels of overthinking. You've considered all the parts where you need to tread carefully. You'll need to be humorous, but not offensive; profound, but not boring; proud, but humble. After assessing exactly where the lines are, you might have paralysed yourself with self-doubt. Fearful of being 'wrong', you can't write a word for weeks. The idea of finding a decent opening line fills you with a desperate urge to throw away your laptop and leave the country.

Before you start looking for your passport, know that the whole process can be far easier than you're building it up to be. You just have to get the foundations in place early. The worst thing you could do is put it off for a few months. Then another few months. Then, a few days before the wedding, open up your laptop to stare at a blank screen for a couple of hours before setting up a WhatsApp group called 'Stories re Steve???!!!' If you're reading this chapter now and it isn't the morning of the wedding, then congratulations, you've already done the right thing. (If it is the morning of the wedding, then good luck to you and, wow, I so wish I could do that.) The moment you know you have to give a speech, start thinking about what you want to put in it. Make notes every time something pops into your head; then when you're two to three months out from the big day, you'll have lots of content and material to play with.

The wedding speech is a favourite part of my job. I am employed in total secrecy to coach and craft, so that at the wedding my client will perform in a way that feels off the cuff. No one ever knows we've been practising this nonchalance for months. The result gives the speaker a feeling like no other. Some clients have told me the blend of relief and euphoria is comparable to finishing a marathon, the plane taking off for a long-awaited holiday, or even (in one rare example) giving birth. The real enjoyment for me comes as I watch them practise, able to see something that they can't. I can see how much the audience is going to shake with laughter, slap their thighs with glee and even cry with catharsis, love and elation. They don't know it yet, but the messages, voice notes and even videos I am sent after the occasion will prove that their words had more power than they ever thought possible and were more evocative than they ever imagined they could be.

Most of all, they don't yet realise just how much the audience is willing them to succeed. If you win, so do they. One thing I have noticed is this: the audience wants to laugh. In fact, they're desperate to. The moment you get that first joke to land, there is no sweeter sound than the roar that comes out of the crowd in front of you. This is the moment you know they're on your side, and the reason I get in a joke as early as possible. Give them an excuse to laugh early, and they'll suddenly find it hard to stop. Days/weeks/months/years later, no one will remember a single word you said, but they'll describe it as very funny.

Before even thinking about opening up a Word document, let's run through a few basics that can lead to a speaker 'missing the mark'. To stay at the right end of the scale, there are six big points you need to know:

1. Keep it short

Once again, the most common culprit of speeches that miss the mark is of course length, with some speakers believing that the longer the speech, the better they're doing. You're not delivering value for money by overrunning. I've never heard anyone say, 'That was a pretty good speech. I just wish it had gone on for longer.' Seven minutes is a great length for a wedding speech; eight is the absolute max. If you've cut it below that, well done. Lincoln's Gettysburg Address was two minutes long. Instead of asking yourself, 'How do I fill this time slot?' Start with the right mindset. Ask, 'What are the things I *absolutely* need to say?' Because once you've stood up and delivered those, the job is done, you can sit down. Fluffing to fill out time only detracts from the good bits. Less is always more. Try saying the speech out loud – timing yourself is crucial to ensure you're not overrunning (and you should be doing this to practise anyway).

2. Avoid in-jokes

The second is to avoid indulging in in-jokes that are guaranteed to go down brilliantly with only about six people at a 200-person wedding. This is only made worse when the speech comes from a duo or a group. I've witnessed group best-man speeches with the script haltingly passed from one speaker to the next. Bad am dram. Avoid this nightmare by imagining the audience is a group of well-meaning strangers you've met in the pub. Would this story be funny to them? If not, cut it out. Remember, slightly amusing anecdotes can be transformed into raucous open-mic-night material through the power of embellishment, exaggeration and blown-up character depictions. If in doubt, test your material out. Stand-up comedians refine their routines by practising the material in low-key venues, running through draft jokes with notepad and pen. If in doubt, run a story past a friend or colleague who can give you an honest response (which should be laughter – if they simply say 'that's funny' with a straight face, don't see that as a green light for a hilarious story).

3. Don't deliver material that will make the audience cringe

A great speech will have them laughing out loud but not laughing *at* anyone. Love should always be very obviously at the heart of your content. Play around, overstate any character traits that might seem unusual to an outsider, but it's generally best to avoid anything that could be considered an outside attack on a marginalised group (e.g. any kind of 'isms' or 'phobias'). A good rule in comedy is to punch up, not down, meaning you can always make yourself the subject of the joke to get a good laugh.

4. Avoid alcohol

A few drinks are fine and may increase your confidence, but be careful not to overdo it – you'll feel a lot more in control of your delivery with a clear head. And if you're the one organising the wedding, it might be best to have the speeches sooner rather than later so your speakers aren't nursing one sad glass of fizz the whole dinner.

5. Props and poetry

Props are helpful for bringing a sense of fun to a speech. I've seen it all: taxidermy, Deliveroo bags, even a copy of *The Legal 500* (don't ask). Tools to surprise the audience empower the speaker. A good example came from a very nervous accountant who needed to do a best-man speech. His comfort zone lay in Excel spreadsheets not stand-up, so he created a PowerPoint presentation (complete with graphs) to demonstrate the increasing equity value of the groom throughout his life. It was a meticulously planned, simple and exceptionally effective speech. Gimmicks can play out brilliantly, but only if they're done well and not half-arsed. It's the same with poetry. Spoken word falls into only two categories: brilliant or terrible. I have yet to see a middle ground. This means, if you're going to do it, you need to do it *exceptionally* well, and that takes serious practice and a lot of thought, otherwise it's just going to look like a cop-out. For example, changing the lyrics to the theme from *The Fresh Prince of Bel-Air* isn't quite as original as you might think. If I type 'Fresh Prince rap wedding speech' into a Google video search, I get back 184,000 results. Stop it.

6. Practise out loud

The big secret to all speeches is the more you do it, the better it becomes. Practise by recording a very rough first draft (without a script), then playing it back to yourself. Do this every day for the next two months, and by the time you get to the wedding, you'll not only feel confident, it'll look as if you just magically came up with something compellingly brilliant on the spot. When it comes to the actual delivery, you're welcome to use notes. Handwritten notes are fine, just ensure they're on index cards so you're not masking your face with a piece of A4. Smartphones have become the modern-day signaller of no longer listening or reading email, so avoid using one at all costs. You wouldn't want someone in the audience to communicate with you while staring at their phone, so don't do the same to them.

You can't half-arse a good speech, but the feeling you get the other side after you've nailed it, is incomparable. You'll be festooned with compliments and embraced. A mini-celebrity for the night. All your hard work will pay off and, most importantly of all, you may even find you've enjoyed the process. Unfortunately, it may also result in you being asked to do it again some day. If you prefer to stay out of the limelight, be careful not to build too much of a reputation for yourself.

The Best Man's/Best Woman's Speech

This can be the hardest of the lot and the one that comes with the greatest level of risk. But remember, strictly speaking, your only official duty is to toast the newlyweds and tell the groom/bride/couple that you love them. If you don't consider yourself naturally funny, then don't try to be – short and sentimental always triumphs over laboured.

Let's do this *Blue Peter* style. To prepare well in advance, gather together the following items:

- One beer
- A book of jokes
- *Debrett's Wedding Guide* (the 1997 version is my preferred choice)
- Pens and paper
- Index cards (the little cue cards that you used to revise with)

HOW TO DO...

If you can't get hold of any of these items, a good substitute is the internet.

Step 1: Open the beer.

Step 2: Start drinking the beer.

Step 3: Start gathering information. What stories do you have about the subject? Write down everything you've got. Ask yourself questions such as: How did you meet them? What were your first impressions? Did you like/not like them? What would their mum say is their most irritating habit? What is their most incorrect opinion? What was the most embarrassing moment of their life? What were they like at school/high school/university? If you still can't find anything, call in the other key players, give them a beer, and ask them the same questions. Once you've a filled a notepad, start to look at what material might work.

First, put a red pen through anything you wouldn't want Granny to hear. Then, working with what's left, choose around three stories that you think are the funniest, and put them in order of mildest to wildest. Anything left you can leave in your back pocket for spare ammo.

Here's one I made earlier about two entirely fictional brothers (who may or may not be speaking to each other right now):

- Stag do – no
- Getting a medal from his nan – 2

- That polo incident – 1
- Vegas trip – no way
- The bet he lost in Afghanistan – back pocket
- Tattoo? – absolutely not
- Fancy dress party – under no circumstances
- Meeting Kanye – back pocket
- Rugby injury – back pocket
- Getting detention at school – back pocket
- Running for the chopper mid-interview – 3

As you make your choices, remember the golden rule that less is always more. That means I'd rather have two or three stories that are really good and delivered brilliantly than four or five that may or may not land.

So now you have three stories, start with the mildest, finish with the wildest:

- Running for the chopper mid-interview – 3
- Getting a medal from his nan – 2
- That polo incident – 1

Step 4: Start to refine your stories. Don't let the details, facts or even the truth stand in the way of honing your content. Go back to that imaginary group of cheerful punters in the pub. How would you deliver these for maximum entertainment?

Step 5: Once you've written your stories down, record a list of the qualities you admire about your best friend. These might include loyal, courageous, fun, kind.

Now make a list of the less than admirable traits. Remember, these are meant to be humorous, not offensive. It's OK to call someone disorganised, but not OK to call them dishonourable. A list of these traits for our fictional groom might include 'messy', 'ginger', 'terrible golfer', 'stubborn', 'rapidly receding hairline', etc., etc.

Step 6: Next in the process is to come up with an opening line. Look at your list of not-so-great qualities and pick out one of them. Now blend that quality into a joke. If you can't come up with your own joke, then use a book of jokes. You can buy lists of jokes off the internet. Make a bland insult humorous by adding an extreme element to it. For example, it isn't funny to say, 'The groom has a receding hairline', but it is funny to say, 'The man who has about three to four haircuts left in him.' Turn this into a decent opener by simply adding an introduction.

For example, 'Ladies and gentleman, for those of you who don't know me, my name is William, and I'm the best man, so please, sit back, relax, and the next three hours should fly by. (Pause because you might get a small laugh here.) Today, my job is to talk about Meghan, the beautiful philanthropist, talented actress and calligrapher – and Harry, the man who has three to four haircuts left in him. (Pause again because there will definitely be some more laughter here.)

Step 7: The emotional bit, which should be easy. Choose at least two of his best qualities from your pre-prepared list and talk about them with sincerity, giving examples of how he is kind or loyal. Then you can talk about how brilliant the bride is, followed by how brilliant they are as a couple.

Step 8: Add a final toast. This can be as simple or as elaborate as you like. Make it heartfelt and brief.

Step 9: Collate your content. You've crafted three funny stories about the groom, the list of his great qualities, the list of his not-so-great qualities. Use the rest of the not-so-great qualities that you've turned into jokes and prepare to sprinkle them liberally throughout the speech.

Step 10: Transfer everything to little index cards. Start to practise the speech out loud. Record it on your phone and play it back to yourself. It will probably sound awful the first couple of times you go through it. But persevere, you'll reach something promising, perhaps even good. Run it, run it again, until you know it inside out and back to front. Don't memorise it word for word, but know it well enough to play around with the delivery. It doesn't need to be perfect; it just needs to be rehearsed.

Once it's all done, congratulations. Bask in your own glory, hit the dance floor, and consider a cheeky snog with a bridesmaid/usher/your other half.

Father/Mother of the Bride's/Parental Figure's Speech

Congratulations! It's a big day for you too and only right that you say a few words. Relish this moment, but I don't need to tell you that the classic mistake here is to go on for too long. We've all seen the speech that reads like an UCAS application form, listing everything from the first recorder recital to the latest insights from their last work appraisal. The other big mistake (and it's rare, but not unheard of) is to treat this like an Oscar acceptance speech. Your content should put heart before the head and not feel self-congratulatory. I've heard of a horror story in which a father of the bride used the opportunity to give a lecture on the best business decisions he'd ever made, mentioning his family only in terms of being a component to his success.

If the speeches are being delivered in the traditional running order (father of the bride, groom, best man), this means you're first up, giving you the luxury of the audience at their freshest *and* you have first dibs on the stories. Think about your role as a parent and what the most wonderful, frustrating, funniest moments of that journey gave you. Add in a few kind words to welcome your new in-law into the family and even some meaningful words of advice. If you need to move from one story to the next, don't worry about seamlessly connecting the two – you can use a simple 'Another event that comes to mind was when . . .' or 'The next story I feel I should mention is . . .' Use these to pull together a handful (two to four) of your favourite anecdotes, interlaced between the thank-yous, and you'll be left with something both entertaining and poignant.

There's absolutely no pressure on you to be funny, so leave that to the best man/woman if you'd prefer. Having said that, I often find that the father of the bride attaches a huge amount of concern to the role because it can also feel like the role of the host of the day. It's worth remembering how the audience is feeling at the moment you stand up. They're slightly boozed up, woozy on love and excited to hear from you, so jump on the opportunity, get them cheering as often as you want. Fix the opening line and the rest of the speech should fall into place. If you don't run over time and simply deliver a montage of the 'best bits', you can't fail. Wrap it up with a big old heartfelt toast and you're done.

A common concern here is that there's a chance you might – er – feel feelings. A question that's often put to me is 'What happens if I start crying?' No matter how many times I hear it, I'm still baffled by this. If ever there's a time that people expect tears, it's during a wedding speech, so if you do find yourself overcome with emotion, allow for it, welcome it. If you feel like it's too much, take a deep breath, look up briefly and take another big breath. Then go back to it, but the good news is, by the time you've gone back to it, they'll either be enthusiastically clapping their hands to encourage you or even dabbing at their own eyes. It's your big proud parent moment, so f**king go for it.

The Groom's/Bride's Speech

Relax, your job is the easiest. You only have two objectives:

1 Thank everyone who is due a thank-you.
2 Tell everyone how much you love your brand-new spouse.

The list of thank-yous should include the following: guests who have travelled extensively to make the event, parents from both sides, the best man, the bridesmaids and, finally, your wife/husband. Traditionally, it is the bridesmaids who should receive the final toast, but these days the fashion is to toast the bridesmaids mid-speech, then finish with the spouse. You're also in charge of 'absent friends', which can be a tricky element. Naturally, you might want to mention those who cannot be in attendance but who would have loved to have been there (although I'd advise against reading out lengthy messages or cards that might have arrived). If you need to talk about loved ones who are sadly no longer alive, do so with sincerity; try to imagine how they'd respond to the day. Contrast dark with light, which will add weight to the heavier part and brighten up the happier side.

When it comes to talking about your other half, authenticity is always the best policy, and self-deprecation in contrast to their brilliance is always well received. Find a balance between the gushing and the hollow by adding in a few humorous stories demonstrating their best qualities. In fact, short stories or anecdotes can provide an oasis among the obligatory thank-yous you'll be delivering. You've got a lot to get through – work only in headlines and stories. It's better to prove qualities than to list them. For example, you could talk about your father-in-law like this: 'He's an empathetic man, well mannered, meticulous, fun to spend time with and extremely warm, etc., etc.' But that's potentially boring, so pick one quality to focus on: 'Michael is one of the warmest people I've ever met. The first time he welcomed me into his home, I knew I was being given special treatment when he stopped mowing the lawn to embrace me. It must have absolutely ruined the uniformity of the lines, but that only made it more special.' Once again, practice is key but, crucially, the delivery must appear entirely unrehearsed here (which, ironically, will take some rehearsal). When you reach the part when you express your feelings towards your new bride or groom, it's important to a face them and address them as though they're the only person in the room. Don't worry if emotions overtake you at this point – that's exactly what the guests are expecting, and it'll only add to the impact of your statement. Have a handkerchief ready though.

Finally, expect the unexpected, but know that whatever happens (or doesn't happen), it all makes up a smorgasbord of memories that will with time become family history.

The first time I was a bridesmaid, I was called to one side by the father of the bride who wanted me to 'run an eye over his speech'. Half an hour before we were due at the church, I was presented with a blank piece of A4 paper with the word 'Amelia' written at the top, underlined twice. Between the two of us we pieced together something in fifteen minutes, including some essential details re the bride's tax return, which was a job her father was keen to hand over to either of the couple. I left him with a handful of bullet points and told him that if he ran through it a couple of times before we went down the aisle, he'd be fine. As I headed back upstairs to carry on with final touches to hair and make-up, I heard the unmistakable sound of his ride-on lawn mower ploughing off into the distance. Despite this, the speech went down a storm, with one member of the audience declaring it to be 'the best father of the bride speech I've ever heard! How did he come up with that hilarious bit about the tax returns!?'

12

A EULOGY

I have written eulogies for people I have never met.

While I don't want you to see me as some kind of grief vampire, I'd describe this as the most profound aspect of my job, and shifting through the swathes of material that make up an account of a lifetime isn't dissimilar to detective work. The objective is to build a psychological profile, a snapshot summarising an entire life – and all revealed in a handful of uplifting minutes. If that sounds clinical, it's because it is, and I never envy the position of whoever has been chosen to carry out the last and greatest honour you can bestow on another human – all within an allocated, pre-approved time slot.

The client tasked with the delivery will turn up at my door as the most cheerful person I'll see that month, either through their maintained brave face or by the virtue of carrying a constant and physical reminder that time is short, and emails are not worthy of any kind of prioritisation. On these rare occasions, our meeting will take place in my home and not an office (too cold) or coffee shop (too public) so that we can quickly feel an honest connection with each other. They see my pile of dirty plates by the sink, and I'll see their grief laid out on the table. If it's the right hour of day for it, I'll offer them something to drink, which they'll (generally) decline, in case it sends them down a path they know they'll struggle to come back from.

Mostly, the client brings me an oven-ready draft and just wants someone to read the script out loud to see whether they can get through it without crying. They stand and deliver the script like a horse-race commentator, barely breaking for breath, before finishing and beaming with relief. The faster they do it, the less they have to think about it. I'll let this happen a couple of times before I offer the same suggestion that I always make, which is to do it once more but to consider the meaning of the words that they're saying. There might be some pushback to this, so I deploy a brilliant line that I've borrowed from local beautician called Helena, who's a waxing specialist: 'Whatever you've got to show me, I've seen it a million times before. Now pants off, please.'

I leave out the last bit.

And then they'll just f**king say it, and they'll cry and, of course, apologise for crying. Some of them recover quickly and push through, and others need something more. A tissue. A hand on their shoulder. Or a good swear. Sometimes, the mere appearance of the little plastic packet of Kleenex is enough to bring on the tears, like a permission slip that says, 'You may show sadness now.'

We'll likely revisit it just once more after that, following some generic advice I give around shortening the third paragraph and making eye contact with the room. Then I promise they can go home, after one last run-through. It's delivered thoughtfully, with a few blinks to hold back the welling in the eyes, and even some smiles in the happier parts. Then they leave, and I know I am unlikely to ever see or hear from them again.

The other type of client turns up without a draft, so I gently interview them for content. Sometimes, I can prompt with a simple, 'So, tell me about the sort of person they were', and have enough material to curate a full biography. As we wade deeper into the anecdotes and idiosyncrasies, I start feeling an echo of their grief. A wave of sadness washes over me for having never met this brilliant person who was so loved, and I make a mental note to call my parents after the session.

Of all the communication challenges this book covers, delivering a eulogy is by far the hardest. Not just because they're tricky to write but, frankly, because you're probably feeling pretty f**king awful. However, as with everything else, there's a formula to follow, which will give you a paint-by-numbers approach to putting together something that will ensure you do the job justice. It's a mistake to believe that eulogies are delivered for the person inside the coffin, when in fact, they're for the people standing around it. You can briefly lift the people in front of you out of the black hole of grief they're standing in. That's why you should always aim to commemorate a life well lived rather than use the opportunity for pure catharsis, even in the most tragic of circumstances. Especially in the most tragic of circumstances. Just like the wedding speech, this is another occasion where you will care deeply about how you perform, and you'll put pressure on yourself to do the deceased person justice. There is no ideal formula for this, no one style or standard. You only have to honour the departed in the best way you know how, safe in the knowledge that they would be forever grateful to you for taking on the task, however you choose to do it. Care about the person, care about the faces in front of you, but care less about perfect performance.

Here's what to do to make it easier:

1. Don't make it a solo mission

If you're not sure what material to include, reach out to the key people and ask them for their fondest memories of the deceased. This is a fantastic activity to do, not only because you'll be inundated with material for your speech but because it often reveals new anecdotes and different sides of that person you hadn't heard about. Don't be afraid to tell the stories that everyone has heard a million times before. There'll be disappointment if they're missing.

2. Find an opening line

As ever, this is the hardest part, so play around with it, and don't let it block you from writing the rest.

There's nothing wrong with stating the obvious. For example, 'Can you imagine the task I have ahead of me? How do I fit a life like [insert name here]'s into the allocated time I have?'

But you can be bolder if needed. The greatest line I ever heard at a funeral was under extremely miserable circumstances. A great friend of mine in his twenties had died in a motorbike accident, and every member of the congregation was really struggling to not break down in floods of tears. After many weepy readings from people who had not been able to shift the mood, his best friend stood up to deliver the eulogy: 'I want to see every single one of you smiling. Come on. Bloody smile! I'm not going to start until you're all doing it . . . Well, this is the worst party I've ever been to, thank God Jamie isn't here for this.' In a matter of seconds, a whole roomful of people had gone from tears of grief to tears of laughter. Every single part of every single person had needed permission to feel happy, for the first time in a long time. It was unforgettable.

Another memorable opener I heard in not totally great circumstances was from a Norfolk sugarbeet farmer, who went with the candid, but appropriate line 'Cancer's f**king awful, isn't it? Sorry, vicar.' If humour doesn't feel right for the occasion, you can simply express how overjoyed the person would have been to have all their nearest and dearest in a room together. Or just start with the date of their birth and go on from there. Read newspaper obituaries if you need inspiration.

3. Cut, cut, and cut again

When it comes to timing, I'd suggest aiming for under ten, and absolutely nothing over fifteen minutes. Remember, you'll be reading slowly, and you can use a script if you need to, so aim for no more than 150 words per minute.

Be ruthless with what you discard, but stories, foibles and quirks will always give a better picture of their character than factual details. And don't feel as though you must include something just because someone has sent it to you. Express your gratitude, but as the curator, you make the final call.

For example, this sounds like a jazzed-up Wikipedia entry: 'Born and raised in the halls of knowledge, my uncle was a product of Applewood School, where his journey of learning began at the tender age of four. It was here that his thirst for knowledge was ignited, setting the stage for a lifetime of academic excellence and intellectual curiosity. At St Edward's High School, he continued to flourish, excelling in subjects that fuelled his passion, in particular mathematics and history.'

But this shows more personality: 'My uncle was a passionate collector of drill bits, which meant he was incredibly easy to buy gifts for. No one ever saw him actually using them, but his ever-expanding collection was meticulously catalogued and ordered. Naturally, his system for organising the drill bits existed only in his own head, meaning that if my aunt were ever to move a single piece or, God forbid, tidy up, she'd entirely disturb their order, and it could take him a fortnight before he was satisfied that each bit was back in its correct place.'

4. Practise, and cry

Practise in advance as much as you can, and then on the day if you cry, you cry. Don't feel that you have to stop yourself. If ever there's a time and a place for it, it's now. If you really want my advice on how to stop the tears, then here it is: the moment you sense that lump rise in your throat, look up at the ceiling and blink a few times, then look back down at your shoes, breathe in, and go back to the script. The other trick you can use is to squeeze the lectern tightly until you feel the lump loosen.

Print the whole thing out and read *slowly*, pausing as much as possible. If it's not too painful, try to look up occasionally and make eye contact with the audience/congregation. A trick I use to prevent rushing is to put a blank piece of paper on top of the one you are reading from. I slowly drag the blank piece down as I read, so that your next line is revealed only once you've finished the line you're currently saying. This ensures you don't rush or lose your place when you look out at the faces in front of you.

5. Address the emotions

It's true that some funerals feel better than others. When you talk about your great aunt who lived a happy and full ninety years, it might not be easy, but there will be a sense of acceptance. More complicated eulogies are where the circumstances are harder to deal with – for example, the tragic death of someone who was in the prime of life. Don't ignore the way everyone in that room will be feeling, and instead try to address the sense of injustice. Find a way to talk about the emotions, but don't believe that it is your responsibility to lighten the load those in front of you are carrying. All that can be done here is to acknowledge the size of the hole in their heart and normalise the intensity of the grief. Acknowledging the pain and paying tribute to the life that has been lost will be the best comfort you can offer.

So now you need to write it. To demonstrate how to do this, I realised I needed a death. Obviously, I didn't want to use an actual client, so I explored fictional characters who, famously, die.

I needed a man of the people. An individual as flawed as he was familiar. So here is how you quickly, quietly, pull together a lifetime in less than a thousand words. Here is how Lisa Simpson would write something meaningful and authentic for the inescapable death of her father, Homer.

> **Step 1:** Find that difficult first line by expressing your own emotions, for example:
>
> *Today I am here to say a last goodbye to a man who meant so much to me. My father, Homer J. Simpson.*
>
> Then, bring in the other party, the people in front of you:
>
> *And while this won't be an easy goodbye to make, seeing so many of you here today fills me with a huge amount of love and warmth, as we come together to remember a man who was our father, husband and friend.*
>
> **Step 2:** Summarise the person in a couple of lines. If you were allowed only two sentences to describe them, what would they be? The mention of flaws and the use humour are not just allowed but wholeheartedly encouraged:
>
> *Dad was a man whose every step was followed by laughter, love, and chaos, wherever he went. He was the very essence of a family man, whose dedication to his children and wife*

knew no bounds, even if it invited catastrophe in on more than one occasion.

Step 3: Now get into the biography. Think about their key achievements or how they endeavoured to make the world around them a better place for others. Link physical achievements to a higher quality – for example, a longstanding position in a company shows loyalty and commitment, just as having an eye for detail demonstrates care and a desire to bring happiness to others. For Homer, that might look like this:

From his humble beginnings at the nuclear power plant, Homer amassed a professional career spanning decades, showing tireless loyalty in his role of safety inspector. But he was not without an entrepreneurial streak – his barbershop quartet 'The Be Sharps' showcased his ability for creativity, performing across the country to countless adoring fans, even picking up a Grammy along the way. He was a surprisingly inventive individual and something of a local hero to many residents of Springfield.

It was his constant desire to improve his community that lay at the heart of every harebrained scheme he came up with. From snowploughing the streets as 'Mr Plow', to self-spinning spice racks, my father was never short of ideas that might make life a little easier or enjoyable to those around him, regardless of the commercial success that did or (more often) did not follow.

Step 4: Now come the stories that show the true character of the man/woman. These need not be flashy or extravagant, they just need to show their raw qualities. They can be the anecdotes that everyone has heard a million times before, or something strictly personal to you, or both, but take a quality-over-quantity approach. A good rule of thumb is to aim for no more than three full stories. Introduce each by emphasising the character trait it demonstrates, and then wrap it up in the same way. For example:

While we did not see eye-to-eye on everything, he always supported my choices, regardless of whether he fully understood them or not. As a lifelong hotdog fan, my decision to become a vegetarian was more than a little perplexing to him. At the time of my announcement, he had become obsessively competitive about barbecuing, which resulted in a cataclysmic fallout between the two of us. On one occasion, I managed to steal the pig he had been planning on serving at a party, which then somehow ended up rolling into a river, where it was sucked up by a spillway and shot far up into the air. Once my father was over his devastation at the loss, he put his own feelings aside to find me, forgive me, ensure I was safe, and even offered me a 'veggie-back ride' home. He would never let his own feelings get in the way of ensuring his children felt listened to and were safe. My father was above all things, constantly empathic to those he loved.

Step 5: Bring in the relationships that mattered most. These do not need to be lengthy, but again, they should show character:

Beyond all of this, his true legacy was as our dad. Bart and I would often witness him being constantly torn between choosing to do what was right and what was convenient, but he always found a way to be the best father he could be.

As a husband, what he lacked in organisation and tidiness, he made up for in pure devotion to my mother. Together, they showed unfaltering resilience, humour and unwavering love towards my brother and me, whatever the circumstances.

Step 6: Start to build a conclusion. Do this by including any kind of silver lining you can find. This can be anything from expressing gratitude towards a life well lived, to knowing their last days were some of their happiest. For example:

It would be too easy to let grief be the overriding emotion today. Instead, I encourage all of us here to be grateful that a man who planned to live a simple, perhaps even 'average' life, experienced so many extraordinary and unbelievable adventures.

Step 7: Finally, lessons learned:

My father did not seek the finer things of life, preferring the smaller pleasures. A cold beer in a hammock on a warm afternoon would suit him just fine. I encourage myself to be happy with the little things every day because of him.

Step 8: One last line. Summarise everything you have said in a single sentence, or simply answer the question: What legacy do they leave behind? For bonus points, tie it back to an earlier reference.

Among all the chaos, the disaster, and the flying pigs, he kept his promises, and made us laugh along the way. I'll miss you, Dad. Thank you for everything.

I hope you don't have to deliver many eulogies in your lifetime, though it can be an enormous privilege, even if it doesn't feel like it at the time. Know that through your words the person is brought back into the room for one last goodbye. You'll almost be able to feel them reading the words over your shoulder, nodding at the reassuring parts, rolling their eyes over the exaggerations, hearing the stories that defined their existence, and smiling.

PART 3

WHAT ABOUT . . .

13

A F**K-UP

So many times, when we want to communicate something important, feelings stand in the way. Fear, shame, embarrassment or pride are blocking the path to saying the one thing that needs to be said. Why are those few words that might just rectify a situation the hardest to deliver?

This was a question I posed to a client who had flown in from Singapore that morning. After all, his job was restructuring, which made him an expert on delivering messages that were in his own words 'difficult to deliver, but harder to hear'. While I wasn't entirely clear on the specifics of his job, I understood his organisation specialised in risk consulting. This meant that his company went in to other companies and told them how to be better companies. And 'better' often meant saying things such as 'If you want to survive, you need to lose fifty people. If you want to thrive, you need to lose five hundred people.'

The man was tall, slick and spoke in a fast but melodic way, with the faintest fleck of a Northern Irish accent running through his voice. He moved like a shadow and travelled lightly, arriving to our meeting with only a small nylon holdall, designed for brief bouts of travel. Previously, we'd had a few sessions online, but this was the first time we'd be meeting face to face, and I was grateful for it. I'd felt as though I hadn't really been valuable to him in any real way yet, and I couldn't work out why.

After a long pause and a deep inhalation, he stares straight through me.

'I don't want to do this.'

Aha. Here is the admission I have been looking for since our first session. I try to stay calm and remind myself that just because he doesn't want to carry on with these sessions is not a personal slight against my credibility. Sometimes it's just the wrong fit. Sometimes it's—

'I haven't been totally honest with you, I'm afraid.'

He brings his hands up to his chin and rests his face on them.

'I asked for your help with delivering a difficult message under the guise that I deliver difficult messages all the time. Well, that's true, but I haven't properly explained why I'm struggling with this one that I've got to do. I have to do it.'

When he explains the task ahead of him, the restrained nature of our previous sessions becomes clear. Here is a man who tells companies all around the world how many employee contracts they have to terminate in order to achieve stability, yet now, faced with the responsibility of informing his closest team member that they're being let go, he finds himself unable to confront the conversation.

There will be no pointers in this session. No scriptwriting or run-throughs. Instead, he will talk to me about how it feels to let someone go, and why those emotions are holding him back from saying what he needs to say. There's embarrassment at the irony, the fear of an emotional reaction, but most of all, it's that guilt that comes with deliberately hurting one of his own.

Of course, the way to face this conversation is to run *to* it and not *from* it. Be direct while acknowledging how the other person might feel. Try to focus on the long-term opportunities they now have ahead of them, all while expressing sincere gratitude.

That doesn't stop it being hard.

This chapter is for those times when you're avoiding a difficult conversation, even though it's the best way to resolve a situation so that everyone can move forwards. One-off mistakes happen, as do consistent mistakes. Sometimes the issue in front of you is your fault, sometimes it's someone else's fault, and sometimes it's no one's fault at all. But before the process of rectification begins, there has to be a moment of acknowledgement. Not all speeches are positive. Bad news, apologies, confessions: these all need to be addressed at some point, no matter how uncomfortable.

I've F**ked Up

I want to say one thing to the American people. Now I want you to listen to me. I'm going to say this again. I did not have sexual relations with that woman,

> Miss Lewinsky. I never told anybody to lie, not a single time, never. These allegations are false, and I need to go back to work for the American people. Thank you.

It is not surprising that the lie heard around the world became instantly quotable, even before it was exposed as a completely fictional statement. The apology that followed didn't quite achieve the same level of notoriety.

On 17 August 1998, Clinton divulged what he had done in a grand jury testimony, before giving a televised statement to the nation, stating that he 'did have a relationship with Miss Lewinsky that was not appropriate. In fact, it was wrong.' A media frenzy followed, and Clinton's hopes that a straightforward confession would somehow put an end to the mania fell apart, resulting in him publicly apologising for the affair a least six times, even going as far as to apologise for his original apology, acknowledging that it hadn't quite demonstrated the level of remorse that had been expected.

'I'm having to become quite an expert in this business of asking for forgiveness,' he said. Extraordinarily, throughout his ongoing statements, Clinton's job approval ratings stayed at around 70 per cent. His personal approval ratings had decreased, but he somehow retained professional credibility among voters. The fifty-nine-year-old president of the United States had been having an ongoing affair with Monica Lewinsky, a twenty-two-year-old intern, but despite his mea culpa moment, the American people were able to separate his personal misconduct from his performance as president.

Who can say how far these admissions of regret went towards upholding his reputation? But someone, somewhere, had to be blamed for all of this, someone who was not in charge of the USA and didn't have any of the resources that a president did. Despite her countless expressions of remorse for her part in the affair, Monica Lewinsky was made the scapegoat in a scandal where one person was an intern and the other person was one of the most powerful people in the world. Years later, in her brilliant TED Talk 'The Price of Shame', she talked candidly about how she became the 'Patient Zero' of totally losing her reputation overnight, on a global scale. It was 2015 then, and social attitudes had gone through a much needed overhaul. She again spoke of how she regretted her actions and again avoided issuing a formal apology. The impact of the talk meant she was able to shift that narrative even further, and go from being 'that woman', to being a person with a voice.

Sometimes you need to need to use the words 'I'm sorry'. Sometimes you don't. And sometimes you need to find a more nuanced middle ground and acknowledge your role in a regrettable situation. Clinton didn't regret the many public apologies that seemingly saved his professional reputation. Lewinsky never used the words 'I'm sorry' in a situation that never should have demanded those words from her. And her TED Talk allowed her to take ownership of her side of the story, explained in a way that made the world see her as an advocate for standing up to public shaming. For both parties, telling the truth became not only an act of accountability but of liberation.

WHAT ABOUT...

*

Admit it. There have been times when you've f**ked up. I know this is true because everyone has f**ked up, me included. The result of that f**k-up is that you either got away with it, or you were held accountable. Why is the word 'sorry' so hard to say?

There are examples of good apologies, and bad ones. The bad ones demonstrate a regret that comes from the experience of receiving backlash and not actual regret for actions. Just look at how Tony Hayward, the CEO of BP, reacted to the BP oil spill in the Gulf of Mexico in 2010. He certainly expressed deep remorse over the damage being done to BP's reputation, but it was his desperate cry of 'I want my life back' that really showed just how little guilt he was feeling over the billions of dollars' worth of damage caused to the environment. Real apologies must show empathy and self-awareness.

If you want to see the best example of a real apology, you need to walk into a room in which a labrador has just finished tearing something you used to value into pieces. The tail between the legs, the head lowered towards the floor, the fleeting eye contact hopeful for some sign of forgiveness, are all authentic expressions of guilt and acknowledgement that they've done wrong. If only politicians were able to do the same.

When you have f**ked up, what should you do to show genuine accountability? How do you say 'sorry' in a meaningful way? It goes without saying that timing is key, and the earlier you can alert someone to the problem, the better. If you've watched any comedy series ever, you'll know that the real chaos comes from when the character at the centre of a wrongdoing tries to cover up their actions, over-explain or sort out the issue on their own. Fess up asap to prevent a bigger problem down the line.

The first step is to make sure you want to apologise and understand that you have caused an issue. If you don't understand that part, the best you'll end up delivering is the false apology, which sounds like this: 'I'm very sorry *if* you were offended.' / 'I'm sorry *you* feel that way.'

Do you see how the person making the apology doesn't actually say, 'I'm sorry for what I did'? They're showing regret only over your reaction. But if ever you find yourself on the receiving end of a statement like this, you should know that you're unlikely to hear anything better, because if the other person doesn't see the issue now, it's unlikely that they ever will. The best you can respond is to graciously accept it as though it were a real statement of regret. Nothing will annoy them more.

You'll also need to avoid pointing blame at anyone other than yourself. Do not lie. Do not give excuses. Do not downplay your actions or make apology videos from your $17,000 per month Manhattan apartment while crying tears of self-pity. This will hurt, but the good news is, if you do it properly, you'll have a much better shot at being forgiven.

Here's how you do it, in best 'guilty labrador' style:

> **Step 1:** Explain. Give a specific timeline as to what happened. Do not be vague or convoluted in your language, just give a concise and clear context to the issue.

WHAT ABOUT...

When you left the house today, I stole your best slippers. I was bored, so I chewed them up and they're now in pieces all over the kitchen. It seemed like the right thing to do at the time.

Step 2: Show the gap. Contrast the mistake with what should have happened retrospectively or explain how it happened. That doesn't mean give excuses, but if it's appropriate to add an explanation, then do so.

Those slippers were really important to you, and you thought they'd be safe under my watch. I guess I just completely lost control of the situation.

Step 3: Say sorry. They need to hear it, and you need to say it.

I knew I'd messed up the moment you came home. I'm so sorry for what I did to your slippers.

Step 4: Show that you understand the impact. This is the really important bit.

I know that this is about more than the slippers. I've broken your trust, and you'll think twice about leaving me at home alone in future.

Step 5: Show what you plan to do going forward. Time and time again I hear managers say, 'I don't mind that they made the mistake. I just need to know they're going to fix it.' Here's your chance to rebuild trust. Yes, you may need the other person's help in sorting things out, but if you show you're already working on a plan forward then you may even find this mistake becomes an opportunity to gain a reputation as being an adult who takes responsibility for their actions and understands the bigger picture.

If there's nothing to be done about the mistake, simply explain that it won't happen again, and outline a future where the issue is no longer a concern.

I can't bring your slippers back. I'm going to work on other outlets for my boredom and see whether I can locate a tennis ball to stop this from ever happening again. I hope this means you can trust me on my own next time.

For Bill Clinton, his version of this (and something you'll hear frequently from people in power) is something along the lines of 'We all need to get over this and get back to working on the important issues at hand.' In the early stages of the apology, this isn't something I'd recommend. Only once enough time has passed should you use this line to politely encourage the other party to move on from what happened.

Finally, don't overdo it, or you'll risk something that sounds grovelling and insincere. A brief but authentic apology is significantly better than one that goes on endlessly and seems over the top.

WHAT ABOUT...

They've F**ked Up: How to Hold Someone Accountable for Their Actions

In my first week of having a real job at a globally renowned PR firm, I hit 'reply all' to an email that definitely should not have been replied to all. Thinking about it decades later still causes me to wince. I won't be the first person to hit the wrong button, and I certainly won't be the last.

Emails go out every second of every day, and not all of them go to the correct place, with the correct content. Just look at the email sent in 2012 by an intern at the Bank of America, who accidentally asked hundreds of internal employees for lunch spot recommendations. A similar incident happened in 2021 when a blank email was sent out to millions of HBO Max subscribers, forcing the company to acknowledge the error publicly and refer to it as 'the intern mistake', sparking a wave of online support and empathy for the intern.

Mistakes happen and, once rectified, can form important learning points. Much harder to resolve are actions that have caused a negative impact, whether accidental, negligent or intentional.

More serious issues that caused heavier impact include an incident at the BBC in 2011 that incorrectly informed every single staff member they would be receiving a bonus, when in fact it was only a few hundred people who were meant to receive the good news. Damaged morale, difficult conversations and outrage naturally followed. Even greater distress was caused the following year by Aviva Investors, a global asset management firm that accidentally sent out an email intended for a single individual to 1,300 employees, informing them they'd been fired. The reaction was catastrophic, creating widespread panic among employees as well as headlines across the world.

I am going to say something that goes against most advice you read in self-help books: if someone goes out of their way to upset you, then it is normal to feel upset about that.

When something happens to offend, hurt or disappoint you, it is perfectly normal to react to that and experience unpleasant emotions. You may feel anger, disappointment or even humiliation. I am not going to tell you that you need to use all of the understanding and love in your heart to instantly forgive what has happened. It is normal to feel anger. However, it's also worth remembering that these feelings are (by their very definition) reactionary, and they will, with time, subside. They're also largely unhelpful, and if you make your grievances your personality, then you will turn this small act of selfishness against you into a much larger tool of self-flagellation.

Don't give yourself too hard a time for feeling feelings, but try not to act on them immediately. An emotional response does not magically absolve you of your behaviour going forwards. We live in the age of the keyboard warrior, where we can instantly air our grievances anonymously, without ever having to do any uncomfortable self-reflection of any sort. Pause. Think. Even briefly.

There is no greater act of self-love than drafting the email you'd really like to send to someone, listing everything your outrage would like to say to them, and then never *ever* sending it.

(This is the really important part – we've all heard a horror story about the person who accidentally hit 'send'.)

Step back, and when you have given yourself some time, try to look at the situation objectively, as a third party might. Understanding the intention here is crucial to getting your head around your own response.

For example: you are boarding a flight and see a person loudly berating a member of the cabin crew for the selection of snacks on offer. Your reaction is likely to be frustration – you perceive the complainer as a bully with an inflated sense of self-entitlement. How would your response change if you knew that the angry customer had just intervened to prevent their young child with a life-threatening nut allergy being served a packet of cashews? Immediately you'd understand their reaction. When we understand the intention behind the action, we see the situation with clarity and start to focus less on who has been 'wronged' and more on the best way of resolving the issue.

Holding people accountable while showing empathy takes clear and careful communication. So when the next unexpected f**k-up occurs in your life, regardless of whether it's your mistake or the mistake of someone you are responsible for, it's important to keep emotions out of things and remain objective as you collaborate a way out of it together. That way, you'll be able to focus on the three things that matter:

1 The issue is sorted, asap.
2 The wrongdoer understands the impact of what they've done.

3 Which means that they will do their best to stop it from ever happening again.

Focus on the problem rather than the person. After all, if your goal is for the problem to go away, then it's likely that the perpetrator is the best person in the world to help you with that. Show them that it's the two of you versus the issue rather than screaming about how they f**ked up, and you'll get a better long-term result. Louis Theroux gets a lot further than Piers Morgan because he wants to encourage an open conversation, as opposed to pushing the interviewee to have a breakdown.

Here's how you hold someone accountable:

Step 1: Explain. Using specific examples, explain in neutral terms what has happened/what continues to happen. It goes without saying that you should prepare the wrongdoer for the conversation and that it should happen privately.

When I came home this afternoon, I found my slippers had been chewed up and were in pieces all over the kitchen.

Step 2: Show the gap. What did you want to happen as an alternative? How did this action miss your expectations?

In leaving you at home on your own, I expect you to be able to look after things. Finding my slippers eaten is the opposite of that.

Step 3: Explain the wider impact the problem has caused.

The bigger issue here is that I trust you to be able to be responsible when I leave you alone. What you've done today will make it harder for me give you more responsibility in future.

Step 4: Ask questions and listen. It's important to show that you're willing to hear the wrongdoer's side of the story. Encourage them to share by empathetically asking questions. You're not doing this to soften the conversation, but it's a good way to uncover any hidden issues and, therefore, solutions. Their answers will also encourage accountability and stop them from becoming overly defensive.

What do you think went wrong? / Why do you think this happened?

Step 5: Suggest solutions. Put together a solution with them, and agree a way forward to make it happen. This part of the conversation is still a two-way street, so try to encourage them to come up with a plan, and don't just give them the answer. That way, you'll be teaching the person in front of you how to learn how to fix future f**k-ups, whether they're the cause of them or not.

Right. How do we fix this?

Not every time will an obvious solution pop up – if those slippers are gone, then they're gone. If the issue can't be resolved, move straight to Step 6.

Step 6: Come up with a prevention plan. This is crucial. If the only outcome of the f**k-up is that it never, ever happens again, then it was a f**k-up worth having. Do not leave this conversation without understanding exactly what both of you need in order to prevent future issues.

How do we make sure the next time you get bored there's something other than my slippers around to distract you? What would entertain you when I'm gone? How would you feel about a few more tennis balls lying around?

Step 7: Reach an agreement and check in. Once you've agreed what they're going to do and what you're going to do, make sure it happens. Even when things are plain sailing again, it's still a good idea to check in on them, not to micromanage, but to ensure everything is going in the agreed direction.

How's the tennis ball situation?

Always Come Clean

Consistently hiding mistakes only leads to bigger issues, turning a simple f**k-up into a clusterf**k.

As soon as you've identified the issue, communicate it to the right people, no matter how difficult it feels and however much

WHAT ABOUT...

you can feel emotions standing in your way. Know the facts, get straight to the point, and prepare for questions from the other side. As much as possible, put across your options for a path forward, while offering whatever support you can. Ask yourself, 'If I was the person I'm about to speak to, how would I want to hear this news?' Finally, remember that there's no perfect way of delivering something that no one wants to hear, so it's always better to just f**king say it than to stay quiet.

We have all made mistakes in our lives, and there's still plenty of time left to make many more. A good way to look back at them is to understand that problems that feel very big and very embarrassing now might not feel the same way later on down the line. My humiliating 'reply all' email may still cause my cheeks to burn, but I doubt anyone else involved can still remember it, or who caused it. In the words of the great philosopher Miss Piggy, 'Only time can heal a broken heart, just as only time can heal his broken arms and legs.' While this book does not condone physical violence, the theme is clear: eventually what feels very big and raw now will become old news.

Look up at the sky. Is it still there? If it is, take a deep breath and try to accept what you cannot change. If the sky is not still there, then you are entitled to a full refund on this book.

14

COMMUNICATING WITH DIFFICULT CREATURES

I can always tell when a session is not necessarily going to be about the person in front of me. It's when a client seems especially concerned to check that the door of the meeting room is locked. We'll be in the smallest room on that floor, right at the end of the corridor, in the one that's hardly ever used. After pulling the handle back and forth aggressively a few times, they'll sit down and start talking. There's a great irony in this conversation: the person I truly need to speak with isn't physically in the room. But their presence will eventually dominate every cubic inch of the space, as they become the sole focus of my client's breathless monologue. They'll tread lightly around their subject initially, knowing that if they go in too strongly too suddenly then I might identify them as the problem instead. 'I don't want you calling the men in white coats,' as one client put it. But in time, it all spills out, and in a mix of relief and embarrassment they go through example after example of behaviour from another person that they see as at best illogical and at worst deeply self-involved. What they'd like me to do is to march out of that tiny room, identify the root cause of their frustration and, with pointed finger, tell them to stop behaving like a complete shit.

Alas, it's not possible. Even if I did do this (and, trust me, I'd like to in some instances), it wouldn't work. The old adage is true. You cannot change someone else's behaviour; the best you can do is to change your own and hope for a reaction in them.

In this chapter, we'll discover what these difficult creatures look like, how to spot their behaviour and what (if anything) you can do when it comes to communicating with them.

The Hookworm

Hookworms are some of the most unpleasant, vicious creatures on this earth. They enter the body through the foot, using their sharp mouth to penetrate the skin, get comfortable inside its carrier and move all the way up to the throat. A hookworm's ability to lie undetected for so long means that by the time you're aware you have one, it becomes extremely difficult to get rid of. They're ambitious, successful and have a serious long-term plan to get to the top.

Sound familiar? If you know someone with an extraordinary ability to suck up to the right people in the right place while steadily bringing those around them down, then you could be dealing with a hookworm of your own. Their behaviour is hard to spot because their most used tool is passive-aggressive communication. That might involve anything from unfairly claiming credit, snide comments or subtly undermining the work of others around them.

Somewhere along the line, the hookworm has learned that direct confrontation has led to negative consequences for them, which is why, at its heart, passive-aggressive behaviour is a defence mechanism. They know that this style of behaviour offers them a sense of self-protection. Over time, the behaviour becomes habitual, and what you perceive as a backhanded compliment they see as them simply expressing themselves in way that feels comfortable. In fact, it may even make them feel strangely good about themselves.

Theodore Millon, a renowned personality-disorder theorist, described passive-aggressive people as 'covert negativists', or people who believed that the 'best way to avoid a direct conflict is to say one thing but do another'. Which explains why to other people their behaviour is so baffling. They are operating only on a very superficial level. For example, they're willing to look supportive when people are watching, but behind closed doors, they make comments that are inconsistent, negative or just downright mean. You'll get lines thrown at you such as: 'I was surprised that your report came back to me ahead of the deadline.'

The best way to deal with someone who communicates in a passive-aggressive way is to bring what they're actually saying to the surface.

WHAT ABOUT...

You should respond to this by exposing the hidden spite inside the comment. Ask them to clarify in a very neutral way, feigning confusion: 'Why were you surprised that my report came back to you ahead of time?'

Be genuinely curious in your tone. They'll either try to back away, like this: 'It doesn't matter. The main thing is I have it now.'

Or they'll try to explain: 'I just think that going by how you usually get work over to me...'

The first option is the more likely response because passive-aggressive types behave this way for a reason – they don't want to fight; they just want to make you feel bad.

The second option means you've now exposed whatever it is that they wanted to say, and you can now deal with it.

If you're met with the first, avoidant response, don't let them wriggle away. Keep trying to dig their hidden jibe out. Try this a few times with lines such as: 'I really want to understand your comment, though. I'm trying to understand what the surprising part is.'

Once what they wanted to say has emerged you can deal with it. Do this by first confirming the 'issue' and then repeating it back: 'So you're saying I deliver work close to deadlines?'

Get them to confirm and then give them a helpful and logical solution: 'In future, if you're concerned with the delivery times of my work, please speak to me directly and I'll see whether it's possible to move my deadline forward.'

They're much less likely to throw passive-aggressive comments your way now because they know you're happy to call them out and deal with them there and then.

Another way these parasites keep themselves firmly lodged in a cosy spot is to claim full credit for work that was either not theirs or work that was very much a group effort. The best way to combat this is to appoint yourself the proclaimer of praise. If you're quick enough to shout out your colleagues when you think they've done a great job on something, this will then prevent or disrupt their narrative of 'Yes, that was all down to me, thank you so much.' While you do unfortunately have to include the hookworm themselves in this, it also means your colleagues will be much more vocal about mentioning your name in dispatches in return.

In short, you create a better environment all round, where positive feedback is given freely and authentically. The next time they go on a secret self-promotion campaign, they'll come across as both inaccurate and immature. A line that still haunts me was described to me by a client who had a very special hookworm in their lives. This individual would famously drop sharp, personal insults but would add the phrase 'hugs and kisses, darling, but—' before they got to the poisonous part.

'Hugs and kisses, darling, but you're not exactly the tallest person in this office, are you?'

'Hugs and kisses, darling, but I've seen better ways to keep a client happy.'

'Hugs and kisses, darling, but you're not considered the brains of the operation around here.'

As this was in the days long before this behaviour would be flagged to HR, my client had to deal with the hookworm themselves. The perfect opportunity came when they found themselves making tea with her, and the hookworm was clearly warming up to drop another 'hugs and kisses' bomb. Before she got even halfway through her insult, my client cut her off.

'Do you know, hookworm, in all the time I've worked here, I've never really understood that "hugs and kisses" phrase. Why do you use it?'

They confronted the hookworm with exactly what she'd always been running from: an honest conversation. The client went on to tell the hookworm exactly how the words 'hugs and kisses' made them feel.

'I didn't do it perfectly,' they told me afterwards. 'But I made damn sure she knew how it felt to be the on the receiving end of her bloody "hugs and kisses".'

The Hippo

Per year, hippos cause more human fatalities than lions, snakes or crocodiles. They're highly territorial, extremely aggressive and have a bite force that can easily crush bones. What has made this cuddly-looking aquatic pig such a complete bastard? How might a therapist put them on the couch and assess why they behave like the angriest vegetarians in Africa? Simple: they've evolved to be that way. Their aggressive behaviour has worked well in the past to get them whatever they needed: a mate, food or territory. When your first method of defence is attack, it becomes very easy to build a reputation that encourages others to stay the hell away from you and leave you to your own corner office.

The office bully knows from previous experience that their behaviour is highly effective. So why would they change? If they know they can get what they want by simply shouting the loudest, they'll have no motivation to use different tactics.

How do you combat the bully? By demonstrating back to them that their tactics are completely ineffective on you.

It's rare for me to work with a hippo. Mostly I am put in front of the person who is directly under the hippo and on the brink of handing in their notice. They have approached me as a last attempt to push back. 'I just need to be more assertive,' they'll often say. This might well be true, but it gets harder and harder to stand your ground when the hippo is consistently roaring in your ear.

When I do get to work with someone who exhibits hippo-like behaviour, it takes a few sessions for them to acknowledge the way that they're acting. One hippo asked me if I thought he'd benefit from an anger-management programme. 'I don't want to shout at people, but it's how I get the most out of them,' says the hippo. When we explore what other communication methods he's tried, he comes to the realisation that there weren't any, so while his tactic of 'I scream "jump" at them and they jump really high' was working, it was also the only tactic he knew.

Here are the three approaches to use to encourage the hippo to try different styles of communication:

The 'Nothing' Approach

When a bully approaches you and tries to engage you in conflict, your best response is to be as boring and as emotionless as possible. Give them absolutely nothing. Here's an example:

> Hippo: I can't believe all the meeting rooms are full! Who the hell is booking all the meeting rooms! I can't tell you how stupid you look right now!
> You: OK.
> Hippo: You're unbelievable! You actively make my job harder; do you know that?
> You: Uh huh.

Also known as the 'Grey Rock Theory', your response is cold, detached and says very little. Eventually the hippo will realise that screaming at you won't get you to kick other people out of a meeting room just because they failed to book one in advance. This is a good technique because it shows the bully that aggressive behaviour won't even get them a response, let alone the thing they want.

Stand Up for Yourself

'Nothing' is a good tactic for when you know that you're stuck with someone who consistently shouts to make doors open for them, but the best way to beat bullies is to stand up to them. Here's how you do it.

Let them have their rant for now. Eventually, they may even start to hear themselves and calm down. But you have a right to stand up for yourself if you are frequently and unfairly the victim of aggressive behaviour. Keep evidence of what you're experiencing in a diary, and then either raise it with the individual themselves, or escalate it. If you are willing to speak to the bully directly, then do so, and express yourself carefully, using evidence. Ask to speak to them in a private setting, and then be totally honest. Explain what you're experiencing in neutral terms, and then state the impact that it's having on your feelings, before finally suggesting what the alternative could look like.

Step 1: Evidence.
Last week, when there wasn't a meeting room available for you, you told me that I looked stupid, and you spoke to me in an aggressive manner, saying I made your job harder for you.

Step 2: Impact.
When you speak to me like that it makes me feel upset and as if I am not a valuable member of the team.

Step 3: Alternative.
Finally, explain an alternative future: I'd really like us to work well together, so the next time you have problems finding a meeting room, come and speak to me rationally, and I'll do what I can to help you. If you talk to me respectfully, it'll help us build a better working relationship.

Find phrasing that works for you, and practise out loud if you need to, but the most important part of speaking up is that you explain what you want to be different. After that, they can accept your points, apologise or deny it completely, but the real proof of change will follow from their behaviour and not what they say in that conversation. The hippo who was considering an anger-management programme came to me because one of the people who reported to him was brave enough to have exactly this sort of conversation. Alone in a room with me, the hippo quietly admitted that it must have taken 'a lot of balls' for them to have said what they said. I asked how the hippo had responded, which was not something he was willing to share, only noting that he regretted it. That person with 'balls' may never know about our conversation but, with time, they will see a different style of communication in the hippo. I only hope that they give themselves the credit they deserve for being the one to call out the change. It certainly won't have felt like any kind of victory at the time.

Be the Adult in the Room

Above all approaches, I would suggest that when dealing with the hippo in your life, you carry the ethos 'be the adult in the room' with you. This is not just a useful ethos – it links to something called 'transactional analysis', a psychological framework developed by Dr Eric Berne in the 1950s. Berne theorised that people communicated with each other while in one of three states: adult, parent or child.

> **Adult:** Logical, objective, pragmatic. Processes information in the present state without influence from the Parent or Child state.
>
> **Parent:** Ruling, judging, controlling. Occasionally nurturing or overly protective. Represents the attitudes absorbed from parental figures in our childhood.

Child: Reflects the emotions and desires and responses learned in childhood. May come across as playful, rebellious or even needy.

It goes without saying that the preferred state to operate in is 'Adult'. The hippo will generally operate in either 'Parent' or 'Child' state. Here's what that might look like:

> Can you please tell me where I'd find that client file we talked about earlier?
> *Adult response:* Sure, it's in the shared drive, under the new business folder. Let me know if you can't find it.
> *Parent response:* It's not up to me to tell you how keep track of files! You need to be more organised!
> *Child response:* Oh, I've got no idea where I put it. Files are so annoying! Once you've found it, can you tell me, please?

This gets more complicated when one person communicating from Parent or Child state encourages an Adult to join them in the less healthy states. Many years ago, I was running a workshop for a group of graduates at a major retail company. Grads tend to be some of the most engaged, intelligent and self-aware groups I meet, so I was surprised when most of them treated the workshop like a classroom. They put their hands up to answer questions, slammed their bags on the desk and generally demonstrated the behaviour you might see from a group of teenagers who've been told they have to spend Saturday in detention. I was absolutely baffled by what I was seeing. The mystery was solved only moments later when a woman with the title 'Talent Development Manager' came to collect them from the workshop.

> 'How are my boys and girls doing today then?! Do you all need a toilet break before we get out the snacks?'

The entire theory of transactional analysis can be explained in one sentence: Treat people as if they're children and they'll behave like children; treat people as if they're adults and they'll behave like adults.

Just because someone is throwing their toys of the pram doesn't mean you should scramble to pick up the toys (Parent) or start throwing toys with them (Child). You can calmly wait for them to return to Adult state before communicating as one adult to another.

The Mosquito

The only creature more deadly than a hippopotamus is the mosquito. They're lightweight, agile and attracted to human sweat. While you might see them as no more than an irritation, their ability to spread disease makes them a serious threat to animals much larger than they are. They're everywhere, and just when you're about to start getting on with things or enjoying yourself, you hear that familiar buzzing noise that immediately makes you put up your guard.

How do you explain to a mosquito that if they could simply leave you be, you'd achieve so much more? How do you explain to a micro-manager that their checking in every half-hour isn't making you work faster? And, in fact, their continual corrections over the tiniest of errors isn't building your confidence but doing the exact opposite?

First, remember not to take this personally. What you've experienced is not simply someone's overenthusiastic approach to management but an unfortunate symptom of someone struggling with control issues. In the 1960s, psychologist Julian Rotter explored the concept of Locus of Control, which distinguishes between two orientations: Internal and External.

> **Internal Locus of Control:** Individuals believe they can influence outcomes in their lives through their own actions and decisions. They tend to take responsibility for their successes and failures. They may have such confidence in their ability to influence outcomes that they feel compelled to take over a situation. This can lead to micromanagement, as they may refuse to let external factors or others have a significant impact on the outcome.

> **External Locus of Control:** Conversely, these people believe that their life outcomes are determined by external factors, such as other people, the environment or fate. Individuals with a strong external locus may often feel overwhelmed by situations where they perceive a lack of control, leading to feelings of helplessness. As a coping

mechanism, they may engage in micromanagement to regain a sense of control.

Those with a strong *external* locus of control cannot trust you because they can barely trust themselves. Those with a strong *internal* locus of control cannot trust you because they can only trust themselves. Add this to some perfectionist tendencies and concerns around how senior people perceive them, or anxieties around unknown factors popping up out of nowhere, and suddenly you have someone who can sleep at night only if they know they have overseen every tiny detail of any project or person that they have access to. Ironically, what this micro-manager needs is careful management, regardless of which end of the scale they're at.

You need to build trust with the manager by first reassuring them that they are good at their job. While it might feel like the last thing you want to do is praise them for their breathing-down-your neck approach, remember that they're doing this because they genuinely believe this is the best possible way to support you. You will need to go on the charm offensive for a brief but intense period of time to build their trust. Start with showing genuine gratitude wherever there's an opportunity to. A simple 'thanks for the support you gave me with that client' is going to start to make them feel more appreciated. You can even subtly remind them of any external positive feedback that confirms the work that's being generated is already going in the right direction.

Then go further in building that trust by bringing them small conundrums for them to troubleshoot with you. This part is essential because you're starting to beat them at their own game by seeking them out before they have an opportunity to seek you out, but you're also showing them that you will happily come to them whenever there's an issue. It goes without saying that during this period, you need to make a real effort to deliver work that is above and beyond the standard they expect from you. Finally, when it comes to communicating with them, reflect back their language to them. That way, you're doing the micro-managing for them. For example:

> Mosquito: We need to ensure the quality of work here is really in line with what our client is looking for from us. I want you to go above and beyond on this one.
> You: OK, so we're going above and beyond on this one. Got it.

Continue this approach until you feel that the manager is starting to trust you, and even loosening their grip on your activities. Now is a good time to have a conversation in which you express to them your big dream of having more ownership of projects. Explain how you really want them to trust you to take on challenges without the burden of them having to check in on you so frequently. That's right – you're asking them to give themselves permission to stop micro-managing you.

Finally, if that doesn't work, take the same approach as above and revert to having a firmer conversation one on one with them. Arm yourself with clear evidence and then prepare a conversation with *Examples*, *Impact* and the *Alternative* and wait to see if there is a palpable difference in their actions.

Any serious behavioural change takes time, and you shouldn't expect instant results after your conversation. This is a big theme with those who continually feel the sting of a micromanager. The main antidote here is to build trust, after which you may start to feel that sense of autonomy you've been looking for. But often the question I'm really being asked is not 'How do I tell my micromanager to back off?' but 'How do I speed up the process of getting them to trust me?' One client who was working with me on this exact issue came up with an approach that while I wouldn't necessarily condone, seemed to prove effective after a few months. Their plan was twofold: first, get better at setting boundaries with their micro-manager. Second, to enter into a silent competition of 'Who can communicate about this first?' The manager would walk over to their desk to talk about a new project, and by the time they were back at their computer, they'd have an email summarising the conversation. The manager would receive a lunchtime update responding to the task that had been set that morning. The manager even received a barrage of messages during one business trip to Barcelona, keeping them informed of airport arrival times, check-in time, security clearance time, the time they'd sat down on the aeroplane and the time that the aeroplane started to take off.

As I say, I wouldn't *necessarily* recommend this approach, but for this particular relationship it quickly established for both parties that constant check-ins weren't strictly necessary.

The client told me that the moment they knew their plan was working was when their boss politely suggested that it might be time for a holiday.

Whether you have a hookworm, hippo or mosquito in your life, there is something to remember with all these difficult creatures. It may feel good to rant about what you perceive as the frankly unhinged behaviour of others, once you've found yourself a broom-cupboard-sized room and you've triple-checked that the door is locked. Indeed, I think it is your human right to discuss the habits, actions and characteristics of others you find completely baffling in private.

It helps to accept that neither of us can solve the problem through this end-of-the-corridor conversation. And in every office in every company all over the world, there is at least one tricky character who's causing the same problem for someone else. Just as you've dispatched one mosquito, another one will pop up, so don't waste too much time and energy slapping the air and thinking that'll stop you getting any more bites.

Better the creature you know . . .

15

ASKING FOR A PAY RISE

'If I'm completely honest with you, I sort of thought you'd have a fedora hat,' I said.

The man opposite me threw back his head and flashed a wide smile, without breaking into a laugh. We were sitting in a buzzy, modern space somewhere near Chancery Lane. It had been extremely well chosen for the purpose of our meeting, which required some level of secrecy. With its glossy black walls, low tables and little tea-light candles, it had all the feel of a private members' club, but because the people here seemed to be holding intensely productive conversations, the setting was far more intimate. Far from having a fedora, the individual opposite me was almost completely bald, with extremely good teeth and a clean-cut look. The rolled-up sleeves of his denim shirt give him just a touch of 'tech-bro', and I felt compelled to admit to him that he didn't look anything like what I'd expected a dating coach to look like.

Some weeks earlier, he had sent me a message asking for a meeting while making it clear that he had a specific business opportunity in mind. Other than this, there wasn't much more information that I could extract: he was insistent that a face-to-face meeting would be the best way to have an effective conversation. I was intrigued – so it was difficult not to agree – and so here we were, in full negotiation, as he put to me a proposition that I'd never received before.

An over-zealous sense of curiosity has caused me issues in the past, so I'd done a thorough ten minutes of research into him on my journey to the meet-up. Nikolas Demir makes one thing very clear in his online profile, and that is that the phrase 'pick-up artist' is offensive to him and his clients, and likely to be indicative of an expensive scammer. What he offers instead, his website says, is something 'distinctly different'. Nikolas takes a small group of men and women and coaches them to be more confident when it comes to talking to potential love interests. His programme is neatly structured and varied and contains everything from photography packages to role-play with actors to seminars. The next cohort has been 'selected', and he is now putting together his greatest course yet. And it is for this, he has told me, that he'd like my help. His suggestion is a workshop entitled 'Seal the Deal – master the art of making contact', which will involve 'expert communications coach' Susie Ashfield teaching his latest group of students how they can obtain contact details from a potential match, before following up and asking for a date.

I briefly thought back to the last time I had actually asked someone for their number outside a business setting, but it felt too fuzzy and too painful to drag to the surface. Instead, I was reminded of the time a few months ago when the man from whom I was trying to buy a coffee asked for my number so that I could remind him of the title of the book I was recommending. I hadn't bothered sending it on, and it only now occurred to me that the exchange wasn't anything to do with the book. I didn't have to mull these thoughts for too long to give my answer to Nikolas. I explained that I was grateful, but the opportunity would be better placed with someone else.

'I thought you might say that,' said Nikolas, who seemed remarkably well prepared for this pushback, 'but it's not that far away from what you do. On your website it says you helped someone ask for a pay rise. Asking for a phone number is not so different I think.'

I asked Nikolas to join the dots for me because, aside from them both being questions, I saw very little correlation between the two.

'The biggest issue for my clients is confidence,' he responded. 'They choose someone, and they put this person so high in their regard that they come to them on their knees, feeling unworthy of their time. I teach them to have a greater sense of self-worth, so instead they are the ones who demand attention. They know what they bring to the table.'

I had to hand it to him: Nikolas was on to something here. The very last pointer that I had given to my client who was after a pay rise was to go into the conversation with the mindset of: 'I am just as valuable to them as they are to me.' And it had worked. Greater than confidence, it had instilled in them a fearlessness of rejection, enabling a collaborative discussion with a successful outcome.

*

Just as self-promotion brings about that 'icky' feeling, our ability to ask for something we want, need or frankly deserve is impeded by the same thing: fear. Asking for the corner office, requesting feedback or asking the person we live with to do just a few more domestic tasks – in most situations, we're frightened of the response we might receive. And there's no place this shows itself more when anticipating the response we'll get when asking for a pay rise. However, we're not as much of a burden as we believe ourselves to be when asking for things.

In an experiment called 'The Estimation of Compliance', the social psychologist Vanessa Bohns set up a study in which a group of participants was asked to estimate how positive a response they'd receive when asking strangers for small favours. Before actively going out and asking folk for directions or if they could borrow a phone to make a call, the participants assumed they'd be inconveniencing the person they approached. They estimated that the number of strangers who would be willing to comply with the request would be very low. In reality, a high number of people assisted them, proving that the requests weren't necessarily as big as the favour-asker had thought.

In other words, there is a psychological barrier when it comes to asking for what we want. We might perceive a specific request as being immediately irritating and likely to be rejected, but that often isn't the reality. The study also revealed that there's a general social consensus that helping other people (especially those in distress) is a good thing.

The old adage of 'don't ask, don't get', holds up. The fear of imposing on others is often overstated. So when it comes to asking for a pay rise, if you're willing to push through that initial feeling of awkwardness, think what you might achieve. Remember that the worst answer you could get is a 'no', which is in no way linked to how the person you're asking relates to you. Asking the question won't damage your credibility. If anything, showing that you have the courage to ask will show you to be proactive and assertive in the way you make requests.

There is no greater negotiator than a five-year-old. Diplomats, business moguls and terrorists have absolutely nothing on these tiny psychopaths who relentlessly throw reason after reason at you as to why they absolutely need the thing that they are asking for. An ice-cream, a plasticky magazine or even cold hard cash, everything is up for grabs, and they have realised that the key to acquiring their target simply involves fighting an adult to the point where they are willing to give in. They have nothing to lose, despite becoming increasingly familiar with the word 'no'. They are fearless in asking, because they know that no matter how far they have to push the request, there's always the chance they might just get what they want.

What is it that these mini-dictators understand that we don't? They are blissfully unaware of the social nuances that we desperately fret about as we grow older. In short, they do not care that repeatedly asking for that thing that they so desperately long for is likely to, well, f**k you off a bit. As we become adults, this switches, and our ingrained desire to live a life where we don't cause a headache for anyone (especially not someone we see as being 'in power') often prevents us from asking for something that would have a huge positive impact in our lives. We need to harness some of that tenacity (without resorting to a screaming fit) by finding a balance between being bold enough to ask and not enraging the other party.

But when it gets to the ask, how should that happen in order to place your request in the best possible light?

The answer is in the art of the 'win/win'. If you are able to deliver your request in a way that somehow seems to benefit the other person just as much as it benefits you, then asking the question will not only feel easier, but is likely to be received much more agreeably. In order to work out where the win/win is, all you need to do is take a step back and ask yourself where the positive benefit to the other party could be. For example:

> **You want the person you live with to do more domestic tasks.** Splitting chores equally creates a better balance in the relationship. Clearly assigning tasks streamlines the process and means cleaning time is reduced. The environment you both share will be cleaner, happier and more welcoming.

> **You feel you are due a promotion.** A promotion now prevents you from having to ask again later, it will boost your current levels of productivity and motivation and

will encourage you to stay in the role, reducing employee turnover.

You need more resources in order to complete your latest project. If you're given more people and resources to help on the client project, it'll mean you have a greater chance of meeting a tight deadline, but without negatively impacting the quality of the result.

If there's not necessarily a way for you both to win, move from collaboration to compromise. If they can't give you what you want right now, what can they offer you? And when might there be an opportunity to revisit this in the future?

How to Ask for What You Want

The hardest part of this is working out what it is you really want before you even think about how you go about asking for it. It could be anything from financial investment in your product/service to a pay rise to simply asking for help with something. Once you know what it is you need, you should then find your 'target', by which I mean work out who the right person to speak to is. But don't just leap into the ask there and then. Arrange to have the conversation at a later date, to give both parties time to prepare and ensure neither of you is on the back foot.

You'll need to start by doing your research and prepping your case. If you're asking for a pay rise, for example, it's going to be incredibly helpful if you know what other people in your position are being paid. Work out what you're worth. Do this by considering what you bring in, recent examples of where you've gone above and beyond and recalling conversations centred around your professional growth (especially important if these conversations alluded to the milestones leading to a promotion). Then break your argument into steps, each of which should have a clear point in support of your request.

Prepare using this formula:

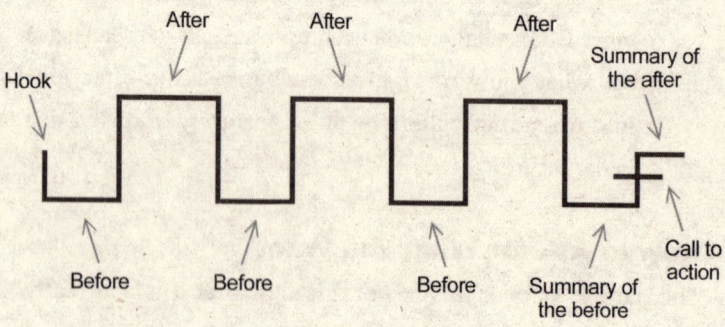

Hook: No point adding unnecessary fluff. Get straight to the point by explaining clearly what your ask is. Explain succinctly what you'd like to discuss.

Before (current situation/problem): In the 'Before', you need to highlight the current situation that you'd like to see changed. Or if there are problems you've identified that you can go on to solve, this is where you outline them.

After (opportunity/solution): The 'After' is a chance to contrast the current situation with an exciting opportunity or offer up the solution to the problem you've just explained.

Summary of the Before: Once you have delivered each 'Before' and 'After', you can start to conclude. Do this by summarising all the 'Befores' that you've outlined.

Call to Action: Explain what action you need your audience to take. Clearly make your request. Be polite, but don't hesitate to get directly to the ask itself. Contrary to popular belief, there is no perfect way to get those words out.

Summary of the After: Revisit every one of your 'Afters'. Take this further by painting a picture of the great future you see becoming a reality, once the request has been accepted and implemented.

Let's use the most common example I help clients with – how to ask for a promotion:

Hook: I'd like to talk to you about my career progression.

Before: The company is growing and will need to take on new hires to keep scaling. Recruiting can be both expensive and risky.

After: Promoting and developing someone who's already showing potential will be a more economical and effective way of keeping up with that expansion.

Before: At the moment, we're stretched. Everyone seems to have a lot on their plate, and it's causing an imbalance.

After: A good succession plan means that if I step up, so can you.

Before: I really like working at this company, and you appreciate me working here, but I can't continue on this current salary. We both want me to stay put.

After: A pay rise would not only stop me from having to look around, but it would also hold me here for longer. You get to keep a great employee; I get to stay at a great company!

Summary of the Before: Currently, the company is growing at a rapid rate, we can't hire as quickly as we'd like, and we're struggling to keep up with the amount of work we're taking on at the moment.

Call to Action: I'd like to be considered for a promotion.

Summary of the After: If I'm given that promotion, we'll be able to take on bigger projects and higher-profile clients. The team will be more balanced, and we won't have to take on any new hires until we're ready for it. I'm a motivated employee with a strong track record of company loyalty, so to keep me here would be a positive move for the organisation. We'll grow together, keep our clients happy and continue attracting new business.

Finally, follow up. Make sure if they do say 'yes' that it happens. If you get a 'no', then take it as 'no for now'. Unless they've explicitly said they don't want to revisit the request, you can come back to it later. Once you've been told 'no', you need to make sure you leave that conversation clear on what's stopped them from granting your request so that you can come back to them once you've worked out a way around it, or the situation has changed.

The most important part in all of this is that you have the meeting, and just f**king ask for whatever it is you want. Practise saying the lines out loud beforehand, but don't put pressure on yourself to deliver them perfectly. 'I believe it's appropriate for us to revisit my salary' might be more refined, but a straightforward 'Look, Steve, I think it's probably time for a pay rise' works too.

You don't need to match the graph above exactly. You can have as many or as few 'Before's and 'After's as you like; just make sure you show both sides. In doing so, you'll hit that 'win/win' that the other party is looking for. The above formula is brilliantly identified by Nancy Duarte in her TED Talk 'The Secret Structure of Great Talks', but the concept can be traced all the way back to Aristotle. You can see it in various iconic speeches, from the Obamas convincing you where to put your vote, to Oprah persuading all of Hollywood to sift out perpetrators of sexual misconduct. Even for the speech widely considered the greatest of all time – Dr Martin Luther King's 'I Have a Dream' – follows this pattern beautifully. The art of persuasion hasn't changed much in the last two thousand or so years, and for good reason.

For Nikolas, despite his well-honed ability to persuade, there was no moving me. Yet among our areas of discord, there was one thing we agreed on: asking for something is a lot easier when you believe there is a mutual benefit to the outcome. As I squeezed my way past the many tables littered with electronics, I considered that I'd be able to catch the last twenty minutes of daylight that were left in the afternoon before heading home.

Cutting through the tourists that were still meandering around St Paul's, I thought about what I would say to someone who wanted advice on negotiating their way to a first date. The best I could come up with was a line I'd heard in the film *The Perks of Being a Wallflower* that goes: 'We accept the love that we think we deserve.' Perhaps the same was true of a monthly pay cheque too?

Whatever the ask, if you go in believing your request is outrageous and undeserved, that's likely how it will land with the other party. As you build up your case, a large part of what you are doing is reminding yourself why you are so worthy of the outcome.

It was dark by the time I'd made it home. And far from the glossy bar I'd just come from, this scene is an entirely different one. The television is on, and from the comfort of a tired and ancient sofa, I begin scrolling through my phone, looking for something that will take me away from the intense discussions of the day – or, more likely, scrolling until I give up and go to bed. But as I shift from image to image, I become increasingly aware that I am being watched. The dog, who is *not* allowed on the sofa, is gazing hopefully at me. I know she is not allowed on the sofa. She knows she is not allowed on the sofa. It is only right that I turn down her request. With the dog overruled, we both settle down in our correct places. It is a matter of minutes before I remember how nice it was yesterday, when the dog and I were together on the sofa, how much cosier it was. How warm it is with her nose over my feet. I go to tap the cushion a couple of times, and as though she has been primed and ready for this exact moment, she lands under my hand by the time I have finished the first tap.

Do not beg for your place in the soft spot. Simply show them what they are missing.

PART 4

I JUST NEED TO KNOW . . .

16

HOW TO SAY 'NO'

Can you remember your third birthday party?

On the date set to commemorate those three loops around the sun, what did you do? Nudity? Screaming? Perhaps you overate and rolled around on the carpet for a bit. However wild you went, I'd still be prepared to bet you can't remember what happened because, like I say, you were just three.

This is the question I'm about to ask the client I have in front of me, who's been holding back tears for most of the session. She's trying to disconnect from her emotions, so she distracts herself by fiddling anxiously with the lanyard around her neck that indicates she's had mental-health training and is 'available anytime' in her role as office counsellor.

I'd been brought in to help her with a pitch that she was delivering to a large American client, and despite not having much time to prepare it, it was in surprisingly good shape. When I ask why out of all the possible speakers in the office, she was the one chosen to do the pitch, she explains that she'd delivered a successful pitch previously, so now she does all of them. Besides, it would help with the big promotion that she has her eye on. I'd simply been called in to try to save her some time. Time, she explains, was a huge issue for her, not just in her office but in her personal life as well.

She runs through her list of extracurricular activities. The PTA, the netball team, the book club, the football and ballet classes for her two young children and, of course, the birthday party for the toddler. The party itself I could understand, but it seemed that every single activity involved in the party came with a host of unnecessary additional responsibilities. The cake, for example, would be a task outsourced to her mother-in-law. But it also meant ingredients needed to be dropped off, discussions would be held to agree the design, and collection would take place a week later. Then there was the bouncy castle. The party didn't really need the faff of a bouncy castle but hiring one would really help out her friend who'd just started an events business. There were party bags (no single-use plastics), and sandwiches (star-shaped) and, of course, she'd need to pick up more chairs, because parents kept ringing her up and asking if siblings could come along. 'Yes,' she said, endlessly. 'Yes, of course.'

It becomes obvious that I'm not actually here to work on the pitch. The pitch is not the problem. We both know it, and now one of us has to say it. The best I can come up with is that question.

'Can you remember your third birthday party?'

And this what it takes. Once the tears have subsided and the true admission of exhaustion is on the table, we talk about the actual challenge in front of us. That challenge is her unrelenting use of the word 'yes'. She believes that this enthusiastic, positive response will keep everyone in her life happy. This one response is the best way to progress her career. This single, terrible word keeps her world revolving.

*

Think back to the last time you really, really wished you said, 'no'. Perhaps it was yet another bloody stag/hen, or a work 'fun' run, or helping your friend move home. Now think back to what happened in those crucial moments where there was a shining golden opportunity for you to use that magic word. What happened? What stopped you? And why did saying 'yes' just feel easier?

History could have been changed if we were all just a little bit more comfortable with being a little bit uncomfortable, briefly. What is it that happens in that moment before we agree to something we know at the time we'll end up regretting? It comes back to that deep-rooted urge this book pushes you to fight against – that deadly desire to care about how others perceive you.

The yearning to be liked by others is, at its heart, not a bad thing. After all, you're essentially saying, 'I like hanging out with other humans. I hope they feel the same way about me.' That need for ongoing social approval has kept humanity going for more than a few millennia now, so it seems only logical to continue to tap into it. The problem comes when it goes beyond an evolutionary impulse and becomes an easy instrument for people-pleasing, which is where the negative side-effects start to creep in. The art of 'keeping everyone happy' is not only an impossible balancing act but also leaves the pleaser in constant fear of disappointing others. Much like the client I have sitting in front of me, they're exhausted from racing around trying to keep as many spinning plates in the air as possible, terrified that one will drop and the whole lot will come crashing down to the ground.

Constantly seeking validation from others makes us overly reliant on their approval and prevents us from developing that truly valuable thing: an independent sense of self-worth. This relentless compulsion can consume us if it becomes habitual, and that fine line between belonging and individuality blurs. In the 1950s, Solomon Asch's Conformity Study showed how an individual would abandon independent thinking in order to fit in with a group mentality. Participants were asked to match the length of a single line against three comparison lines, a question that should have been easy to answer, but actors hidden within the group deliberately and openly gave an incorrect answer. Because of this, the actual participants went along with the majority, happily providing a wrong answer for the sake of 'fitting in'. The experiment demonstrated that social pressure was incredibly powerful, resulting in 75 per cent of the participants conforming to group thinking. In essence, we say 'yes' to fit in, to avoid conflict and to keep the peace. Our desire to be liked leads us to agree to things we probably shouldn't, even when it goes against our personal judgement.

The examples of when 'yes' should have been 'no' are endless. And it's not just mere mortals who live with the pressure of trying to please everyone. Prince Andrew certainly shouldn't have said 'yes' to that disastrous interview with Emily Maitlis that resulted in him having to step back from public duties, despite his belief that it would be a golden opportunity for him to set the record straight with the British public.

Rafael Nadal, one of the greatest tennis players of all time, has expressed regret over not pushing back against a rigorous training regime he adopted so early in his career. While his intense work ethic was no doubt a vital part of his success, it also led to a series of injuries that impacted his longevity in the sport.

And then, of course, there's the man who made the whole world laugh while hiding his own inner emotional turmoil. Robin Williams spoke about the constant pressure he felt to make his audience happy, never breaking character or revealing his true self, even in personal interviews. This relentless need to be 'on' came from not just the sky-high expectations of his audience, but also the never-ending pressure to remain relevant: 'In one two-year period I made eight movies. At one point the joke was that there's a movie out with*out* you in it. You have this idea that you'd better keep working otherwise people will forget. And that was dangerous. And then you realise, no, actually if you take a break people might be more interested in you. Now, after the heart surgery, I'll take it slow.'

When it comes to my own clients, that same pressure hits just as heavy, but with differing results. There's the CEO who just wakes up one day and tells me he's 'lost it'. He can suddenly no longer talk to his employees, make a decision or even send an email without second-guessing himself. When I ask him what he thinks is happening, the best way he can describe it is with the line 'The higher up you are, the further you have to fall. And it feels like all I can do right now is look down.' There's the celebrity chef who used to be witty and charming in all her media appearances, but now she's shying away from the camera. She doesn't want to be a 'celebrity chef' any more (much to the angst of her agent). She just wants to go back to where she started – cooking in a kitchen in Somerset with no one watching. She won't even greet guests as they pour through the doors of her restaurants, having been on waiting lists for months to watch her at work. Mostly though, it's the clients who pull me in because if they'd chosen a therapist, they might hear words that they are not yet ready to hear, such as 'burnout' or 'fatigue'.

If regrettable yeses can happen to celebrities and public figures, then they can happen to the rest of us.

By contrast, when Steve Jobs had the offer of becoming the CEO of Dell put to him in 1995, he declined so that he could continue his work at NeXT. This rejection was a pivotal moment for Jobs, and it meant that in 1997, when Apple acquired NeXT, he was able to go on to make history.

It's important to remember that saying 'no' might receive public ridicule or scorn. Saying 'no' rarely comes with applause. It will not give you mass popularity. But it does give you an opportunity to stand up for what you believe in, and (as the 'thought leaders' of LinkedIn would say) stay 'true to your authentic self'.

For some, adopting this position will result in more than a hashtag-loaded post on social media. In fact, you may need to prepare to make a significant sacrifice. In 1967, when Muhammad Ali refused to be drafted into the US Army to fight in the Vietnam War, citing his belief system, he was stripped of all his boxing titles and banned from the sport for three years. Despite huge backlash, Ali dispensed the last blow when, in 1971, the US Supreme Court overturned his conviction, ruling that he'd been improperly denied conscientious objector status. He made a legendary come back, regained all his titles, and his stand against the draft became emblematic for fighting for what you believe in. Good things can happen when you say 'no'.

So how do you do it? How do you master the word itself?

Let me start with a shocking fact.

You are allowed to say 'no'. Just 'no', in all its full naked glory. Let me show you an example:

A: Can I have a million pounds?
B: No.
(*Fin.*)

You do not need to explain yourself, justify your decision or promise that you'll agree to it later. You're talking to a grown-up, which means they'll be able to handle it, and they'll reach their own conclusions as to why you've given a 'no' as your response.

But this is an advanced 'no'. If you want to start at the entry level, there are different ways you can start pushing back and setting boundaries.

Here are your other options:

1. The polite 'no'

The easiest 'no' to start using is one that is polite but not apologetic. For example, saying, 'I'm really sorry, but no, I can't', feels passive and somewhat defeated. It may even lead to more questions. Add in a note of gratitude instead, which makes your rejection sound positive: 'That's a very kind offer, but no, thank you.'

2. The practical 'no'

If you can add in a genuine practical reason for your answer, then you'll have put together something really solid. It's ideal. For example:

> A: Can I have a million pounds?
> B: I'm very flattered you asked me, thank you! I'm going to have to say 'no', though, purely because I actually don't have that amount of money.

This practical response also works well when someone wants you to be part of their plans:

> A: Can you join us on the charity fun run next Saturday?
> B: I'd have loved to, but I already have plans that day.

The danger here is that the other party interprets your polite decline not as a genuine rejection but a mere practical block, resulting in them responding, 'No worries. What about next Saturday then?' This explains why it is always better to be brave and not dole out a dodgy excuse. A simple 'To be honest with you, running just isn't my thing' will work out better for both of you in the long term.

3. The win-win 'no'

The trick here is to make the 'no' sound as though there's a positive benefit to the other party in your rejection. If you can make your response sound like a win for the asker, then it's going to be a much easier conversation for both of you:

> A: Can I have a million pounds?
> B: Honestly, you wouldn't want it. I've heard horror stories about lottery winners, and I wouldn't want you to change from the amazing person you are now. I'm really flattered you asked me though, so thanks!

Somehow, my rejection has worked out really well for both of us. You go away having avoided the curse of the lottery winner, and I don't have to find you the money, despite giving off the appearance of someone who has that kind of cash going spare.

Here's a more realistic example of how you turn a 'no' into an advantage for the asker:

A: Can you take on this project for me, please? It would really help me out.

B: Thank you for asking me – I love new challenges. I wish I could, but I don't have capacity for that at that the moment, and I wouldn't want to do a rushed job of it. I know how much you value a well-thought-out result.

Fantastic news – the asker has just avoided having a shoddy piece of work being handed back to them, and you don't have to take on something you physically cannot accommodate.

You can even go further and add in a concession – while you don't want to promise anything you can't deliver, this little adjustment means you walk away receiving credit for your response while still firmly pushing back. For example: '... but if my schedule frees up, I'll let you know. I just can't say "yes" to that right now.' Or if you can do it, just not immediately, then push back: '... but I could find some time tomorrow morning. When's the latest you need it by?'

This response tells the other party that you really want to help, but it's just not possible with the amount of work you have and the number of hours in the day. By offering an alternative solution, you demonstrate your boundary but also express a desire to help them out.

4. The empowering 'no'

There are times when you really, really want to say 'yes' to someone, but you know you can't. How do you make sure they don't feel dejected and demotivated by your 'no'?

The most obvious example here is the request for a pay rise. You have a member of your team who's desperate for that promotion, and while you absolutely relish their ambition, you just know they're not ready for it.

Prepare for the conversation like this:

Step 1: Acknowledge the reasons for the request.

I understand why you want this, and I'm very pleased that you're so ambitious. I respect that about you, and I know that a promotion is an important part of your progression.

Step 2: Give reasons for declining.

I really do want to grant this to you, but you're not where I need you to be at the moment in order for me to say 'yes'.

Step 3: Add in *specific* examples.

For example, on our last project, the client said they didn't feel that you were responding to their issues with practical solutions. The role you're applying for requires a proactive problem-solver.

Step 4: Offer alternative solutions.

I want to support you as much as I can in your next steps. I fully believe you can get there, so what I can do is take you through the specific milestones I'm looking for you to achieve to reach that promotion.

Step 5: Establish (specific) next steps together. This is a two-way conversation, so get their input until you've both agreed a clear path forward:

Ok, shall we agree to the following before we review the position on a promotion? You do x *by the end of this month; you achieve* y *in six months; I will see an increase in* z *by the end of next quarter.*

The beauty of a 'no' like this is that while you have turned down their request, they feel as though you're on their side and that you are willing to help them work towards their big dream. Much better than shooting them down in flames, because they're going to come away from that conversation willing to work harder than ever. It should go without saying that you have to be willing and in a practical position to uphold your side of this conversation. False promises are going to work beautifully for now and create serious problems later on down the line. When/if they do reach those milestones, you need to be in a position to promote them to show consistent leadership.

What is harder is declining a request when you know there are practical blocks in the way. For example, how do you say 'no' to someone's request for a pay rise due to financial restraints within the company, even if you know they deserve it? It might not be a comfortable conversation but, as ever, honesty and transparency are key. Be brave enough to explain those blocks clearly to them. They might not take the admission well (which, putting yourself in their shoes, you'd understand) but in the long run, they will come to appreciate your honesty, even if they don't show it there and then. It's the least you can do.

On top of that, a sincere acknowledgment of the work they've been doing, encouraging an open dialogue and showing an understanding of how they're feeling all help to make a difficult conversation easier. Do what you can practically to show your support – are there any job-title changes or training opportunities you can offer them? Finally, don't forget to check in and keep that candid conversation going. By openly supporting their career development, they're going to recognise you're doing what you can to help them, regardless of the barriers.

*

The next time I see my client, she tells me she has cancelled the party. No one is disappointed; no one is upset. The day has been reduced to immediate family only, and while her mother-in-law will bring a small cake, there will be nothing that requires any more organisation, running round or enthusiastic 'yeses' that should have been 'nos'.

Her toddler will not remember their third birthday, but even if a memory were to form, it wouldn't be a disappointing one. Years later, when the child looks back on pictures of the day, they will see balloons, presents and themselves as a tiny, beaming splodge. Despite the absence of a bouncy castle, there will be videos of family members taking it in turns to play peek-a-boo, and even a mischievous older sibling making fart sounds again and again, causing endless snorts of happy laughter.

Saying 'no' hasn't taken away anything from the people who really matter. It hasn't led to a disaster or resulted in an event that was somehow less than what it could have been. The party is simply different, much more manageable and a day that my client will have time to cherish.

17

HOW TO DISAGREE

In the winter of 2015, a woman called Cecilia Bleasdale from a small village in Lancashire, was shopping in an outlet store, hoping to find the perfect outfit to wear at her daughter's upcoming wedding. She considered three options and, in need of a second opinion, took a quick photo of each on her phone so that she could send them to Grace, the bride. Grace considered the dresses before asking her mother which one was her favourite.

'The third one,' said Cecilia.

'Oh, the white and gold one?' came the reply.

'Er, no. The blue and black one.'

'No mum. That's white and gold. And if you think it's blue and black then you need to go to the doctor.'

To continue the debate, a family friend put the picture online and, within a few short days, an overexposed picture of a dress brought the internet to its knees. At the height of its fame the dress was being tweeted about 11,000 times a minute, totalling over 10 million tweets across a week (that's roughly the entire population of Sweden). Celebrities and companies hoping to piggyback on the trend waded into the debate, with Kanye West stating he saw the dress as blue and black, while Julianne Moore saw it as white and gold. For reasons that remain unclear, David Duchovny saw it as teal.

Psychologists, neuroscientists and optometrists weighed in, explaining the phenomenon that was causing people to perceive the same image in two totally different ways. Dr Bevil Conway, a neuroscientist, highlighted how the brain's visual system adapting to different lighting conditions leads to colour-perception discrepancies. Dr Andrew Wood, a psychologist, explained how colour perception could be influenced by personal biases, previous experience and context. Later, Dr Anya Hurlbert, a colour scientist, conducted a study into 'The Dress' and concluded that the brain adjusted the identification of colours through the perception of lighting conditions, known as 'colour constancy'. Expert advice was pouring forward from every and any university worth its salt and, for a brief moment, the entire world had been distracted by a mundane argument that was as universally accessible as it was facetious. But while the majority of people were busily answering the question, 'What colour is this dress?', very few were willing to ask the question, 'Does it matter?'

Here is the perfect example of how debate can be used to unify. We often run from arguments, quoting tried and tested adages, such as 'pick your battles' and not making 'mountains out of molehills', but to feel comfortable enough to stand your ground when it matters (more so than about the colour of a dress) is an invaluable and rare skill. Even rarer is to stand your ground while feeling entirely uncomfortable.

A viral debate about a photo of a dress tells us that when the stakes are low, more people are willing to get involved in the fight. When it was unanimously established that the dress was blue and black, *not* white and gold, and definitely not teal, families, friends and internet strangers felt connected with each other, not torn apart. But this example of unification feels rare when now, more than ever, social media drives our discourse, and this ability to argue good-humouredly about low-stakes things seems to be disappearing – more and more people are ready to hurl the worst insults they can think of over things as small as a misplaced comma.[1] It is easy to be angry on the internet, where (1) you can stay anonymous, and (2) you don't know the other person on the end of your attack.

So here is the dichotomy: cruelty via a keyboard is on the rise; meanwhile, in the real world, people daren't put forward an opinion that feels even vaguely provocative. A client in the public relations industry had been asked to deliver a talk on 'The impact of unexpected political events on fast-moving consumer brands'. They came to me after his slides were checked by the Diversity, Ethics and Inclusion adviser, who concluded that referencing any political event within the talk would be 'problematic' and asked that all references to political events be removed. Delivering a talk on political events without mentioning any was impossible, so the

---

[1] Start by remembering this new take on an old saying: 'If you can't say anything nice, then you certainly shouldn't bother typing it.'

talk was pulled. This is the worst possible outcome: by avoiding sensitive topics entirely (before anyone has even had a chance to complain about them), we miss out on meaningful discussions that could foster insight and understanding.

How do we bring back the art of disagreement (about anything) when my clients seem more fearful than they ever have been of saying something that offends someone, somewhere? The answer is to recognise that we're not actually afraid of arguing but of feeling feelings that we don't enjoy. Resentment, rage, rejection – within ourselves or from the person with whom we disagree. This stops us from having the argument in a brave and effective way, such as through a private, face-to-face conversation. Instead, many of us choose passive-aggressive routes or avoidance tactics that get us nowhere.

If you find yourself avoiding debate for the sake of an easy life, you're going to end up with all the authority of Winnie-the-Pooh. Sometimes a disagreement can be the healthiest way forward, and if you're willing to debate your ideas with someone who sees things differently, you're both going to find something useful in it without letting your emotions take over. That doesn't mean you should ignore your emotions completely, but if you can focus on the facts over the feelings, then you'll get closer to a compromise or collaboration.

Look at the groundbreaking work of psychologists John and Julie Gottman. John conducted his research in the 1980s in a space famously known as 'The Love Lab'. By studying the way couples argued, he and his colleagues were able to predict whether a couple would stay together or break up with over 90 per cent accuracy. By observing thousands of couples fighting, the team gathered invaluable data that pointed to one thing: healthy conflict wasn't just an inevitability, it was crucial in maintaining a long-term relationship. Couples who were able to communicate effectively during conflict would come out of the disagreement stronger. But those who engaged in unhelpful styles of communication during a fight would find that it had a negative impact on their relationship. As Julie, who has collaborated with and been married to John for over thirty-five years, put it, 'It's not *if* we fight that determines relationship success, it's *how* we fight.' Together they founded the Gottman Institute in 1996, describing four key indicators that were essentially a checklist of unhealthy communication styles during a disagreement. These 'Four Horsemen of the Apocalypse' – criticism, contempt, defensiveness and stonewalling – all signalled that without swift rectification, there was likely to be a breakdown.

So how do we engage in conflict in a healthy way? What does bad fighting sound like? What does good fighting sound like?

I work for one company that sits right next to a sweet shop that I constantly find myself slipping into, loading up on dolly mixture and fizzy cola bottles, because I will definitely need the sugar for the session I am about to go into with one of two clients I have in this building. Initially, I was brought in to help one with improving their assertiveness with clients and the other for pitching practice. But after only a short space of time it became clear that both parties had a more pressing subject to talk about: each other.

Let us call these two Simon and Garfunkel. Another pair who, had they not fallen out so spectacularly, could have continued making incredible music together.

Simon describes himself as 'shy'. Whenever he senses that Garfunkel might be in a bad mood, he keeps his head down and stays out of the way as much as possible. From just a few conversations, I'm not convinced that the self-diagnosed label of 'shy' quite fits. In no time at all, Simon is able to talk openly and unreservedly about his thoughts. In fact, in the safety of a private room and with a pile of jelly babies in front of him, he is quite happy to share his feelings with me.

Garfunkel was the one who recommended to his manager that Simon come to me for training in the first place. 'Simon's terrified of speaking up,' he tells me. 'If the building was burning, I wouldn't hear from him about it until my desk was on fire.' This is easy to believe when Garfunkel's reaction to the same situation would be to scream the building down at the first smell of toast and then use any remaining air in his lungs to blame Simon for a blaze that hadn't even appeared yet.

Simon feels that his softer approach with clients ultimately creates a better relationship in the long term. Garfunkel sees this as at best lazy and at worst avoidant. New business opportunities are lost, in his eyes.

Garfunkel's way is more emboldened, more proactive. He's good at pitching and even better at sales.

Simon sees him as insincere and occasionally explosive. He puts style over substance.

Neither party is right; neither is wrong. Both are successful professionals in their own way. The clash is in their extremely different styles of communication. Count them up: all four horsemen are present.

When the inevitable conflict happens, Simon will agree to disagree to try to avoid the fight altogether. He stays silent as Garfunkel kicks off and will continue being silent for the next few days. If he does sense that there's even the smallest chance he's about to be blamed for something, he'll immediately become defensive. Meanwhile, Garfunkel will raise the issue even before it's really an issue and has absolutely no problem expressing his feelings loudly before finding someone (usually Simon) to blame.

In their sessions, they both look to me to confirm that they are right, and the other one is wrong. Neither of them knows that I am seeing the other (which causes some logistical challenges). Strangely, this isn't the first time I have been mistaken for someone who can play the role of a couple's counsellor in my career. I wonder if it would have been worth bringing them into the same room, to sit on the same sofa and share a packet of sweets together. I leave this decision to their manager and instead talk about the healthiest way to communicate the next time there's a 'fire'.

Before you enter into a disagreement, there are a few things to keep in mind:

1. Focus on the problem, not the person
With time, if they are not careful, Simon and Garfunkel will come to loathe even the smallest thing about each other.

In painting such a vivid mental picture of who that person is, you will essentially label them as some kind of office-based demon. The way they chew will annoy you, the way they walk into the room will irk you, and even, in one severe case, the way they breathe will be yet more evidence that they are the most selfish person on this earth. When you hear yourself saying the words 'always' and 'never', then there's a problem: 'You always blame me!' or 'You never network with clients!'

You've not only decided who that person is but also that nothing can been changed about who they are. As tough as it may be, taking a fresh approach every time there's a problem will allow you to see them as a collaborator, not a catalyst.

2. See the good in them

Yes, they do things very, very differently from you. That's probably why your manager encourages the two of you to work together so frequently. While it may take a lot of effort, think about one genuine compliment you could give the other party. And when I say genuine, I mean a compliment that you believe. Thinking about just this one part of them that you truly respect will help you understand them better as a person.

> *I like the consistency you show our clients. I notice how much they trust you, and it impresses me.*
>
> *I am in awe of the way you work a room. Generating new business from one event is really inspiring.*

When you're in a position to deliver your compliment with sincerity, do it. Even saying the words out loud will remind you that they're not all bad if you truly believe your own statement.

3. Be accountable

When you know there's a problem, and you know what role you played in that problem, own up to it. You don't have to be subservient about it, but being brave enough to put your hand up and show acknowledgment will break the cycle of defensiveness you've gotten stuck in and help encourage accountability in the other party too.

4. Take time

Any healthy conflict that happens should happen proactively, not reactively. If you've been dragged into an argument that you're not ready for, explain that you need more time or more information for the conversation to be useful to either of you. You'll be able to have a much calmer discussion, and it'll give both parties more space for listening and understanding. (Insert 'Bridge Over Troubled Water' reference here.)

With those points in mind, here's how to have the disagreement:

> **Step 1:** Prepare for the conversation. Think about three positions: how they see it, how you see it and how a neutral bystander would see it. Put together your argument, but take some time to pre-emptively think about theirs.

The more time you spend thinking about their side of the argument, the more constructive the conversation will feel. Also explain to the other party that you'd like to talk to them about something so that they don't feel on the back foot when you approach them.

Step 2: Now you have to put together whatever it is that you want to say. Keep it brief and clear. You can even script it if that helps. Start by acknowledging the opinions of the other party and even saying what you think is especially good about their view.

Step 3: Contrast this with your opinion, using the words 'I feel' to kick off your statement. This will make your message harder to push back against. For example, if I'm standing outside in the snow wearing a bikini and I say, 'It is warm', then it would be very easy to prove me wrong. In the same circumstances, if I say, 'I feel warm', you're going to struggle to correct me because you can't tell me how I feel.

Step 4: Now you need to put your point across. Just f**king say it and understand that while it might not prove to be correct, it does explain your side of the argument, and it is worthy of being listened to. Make your point with proof, examples or show historical consistency. Be clinical about it. For example:

I feel warm, because I've just stepped out of a boiling hot sauna with a temperature of 87 degrees. I've found that it takes my body a long time to acclimatise.

Step 5: Your next step after this is to seek clarity on the other person's opinion. Aim first to understand exactly where they're coming from. Asking questions that probe the less clear areas of the other person's argument is the best way of weakening their argument, especially if it allows you to identify any technical mistakes, inaccuracies or holes in their knowledge.

Use questions to dig down into what they're really reacting to, such as 'Can you walk me through your reasoning?', 'What do you think is going on?', or simply, 'OK, tell me more?'

Step 6: Provide either a bottom line or a compromise. If you really do want or need to stick to your guns, repeat your bottom line and don't move from it, all while acknowledging their side of the argument.

I understand you're cold, but I am still warm. I don't feel ready to go back into the sauna.

If you're happy to compromise, then great! You've had a useful argument. Clarify what the compromise is and the steps you'll both take to make sure it happens. For example:

You feel cold, and I feel warm. You jump back into the sauna while I stay outside, and when I've cooled down, I'll join you.

Step 7: For bonus points, find the areas that you agree on and pull them together to find a silver lining. For example:

Well, at least we know we have very different body temperatures. We can use this information to be more understanding of each other in future. Maybe our next holiday should be a trip to Switzerland in the spring?

If it is the other person bringing the fight to you:

Step 1: Breathe. Do not put pressure on yourself to come up with a sharp comeback: that rarely happens outside the movies.

Step 2: Instead, if you're met with a sudden flare up of emotions, listen, and pause. Keep listening until you have a clear understanding of the issue.

Step 3a: If you discover you are at fault, then a genuine apology is your next smart move. Stick your hands up to an honest mistake or explain the context or circumstances that led to the error. Once you have genuinely apologised, explain what you're going to do to rectify the situation.

Once you've both agreed on your next steps to sort out the issue, this does not give the other person carte blanche to continue endlessly screaming at you, so disengage if they're arguing for the sake of arguing.

Step 3b: If you're not personally at fault, first respond with empathy. Surprise them by not fighting but listening and using short phrases such as 'I understand that', or 'I see that'. If this doesn't encourage them to work on solutions with you, quickly find a way to express your understanding of the situation and stick to it. You don't have to have the last word to win an argument, but you'll feel better knowing that you both gave them space and landed your point of view. For example:

I understand you're cold, but I feel really warm, which is how I always am whenever I step out of a sauna. I feel like I should stay out here in the snow a bit longer before I join you again because I want us both to be comfortable.

With time, Simon and Garfunkel built a relationship that felt altogether more collaborative and much healthier, which meant that they saw less of me, and I saw less of my dentist. When I last spoke to each of them, they'd put their personal grievances aside and made an agreement to talk more, even if they didn't feel like it. This was especially useful when tensions started to creep in, and that fear of feelings was lurking above them. They'd learned that avoiding negative emotions was neither the goal, nor was it possible, but rarely were those feelings anything to do with the other party. Their different styles didn't diminish their value to one another.

An innocuous argument over the colour of a dress is proof that the world is more capable of healthy disagreements than it believes itself to be. Before their separation, the real Simon and Garfunkel created some beautiful music together, proving that creative tensions can result in smash hits and, as I write this, the Gallagher brothers are still going ahead with their 2025 tour, proving (we can but hope) that reconciliation is always possible. I will leave you with a final question that you don't hear as often as you should:

When was your last, great disagreement?

18

HOW TO GIVE FEEDBACK

'Just tell me what the f**k it means.'

I consider how to answer the very angry client in front of me. He's about my age and has what is normally a gentle face, with those tortoiseshell, 1950s-style glasses. But he's glaring at me with fury, one hand chopping down onto the desk in front of us while the other hovers dangerously over a keyboard. We've been working together for a few months now, but this session has somewhat derailed, and I'm being shown a side of him that I haven't met previously.

He jabs a finger towards his computer screen, and I do a quick scan of a document that feels familiar, with one noticeable difference. Instead of the usual corporate jargon I'm familiar with, smiley faces and emojis have replaced actual words, suggesting that either the sender cannot comprehend anything outside a cartoon format or that they cannot read.

I pause briefly, reminding myself that this anger is not directed at me, even though that's not necessarily how it feels at this moment.

'I have to say, I haven't seen a performance review sheet like this one before. What are the little symbols for?'

But, it turns out, it's not the icons that's he's irate about. He draws my attention to the single line of feedback that has prompted this meeting. It is written into a little box that has a sad face at the top of it, which would normally be written up in the English language as 'Areas for Improvement'. The killer line simply reads: 'Try to be more confident with clients! ;-)'

You'd be amazed at how often this line comes up in sessions. It hangs in the air unsupported, without context and delivered with absolute fearlessness. The commenter knows there are very specific things they'd like to say, but they fear the reaction of the recipient. In using this one line, they've encompassed a lot of specific concerns under one cosy blanket, which they assume will feel warm and snuggly to the receiver. The trouble is, it's completely meaningless, and like a relative with good intentions who tells you just before Christmas lunch that you're 'looking tired', the comment is going to be interpreted in the worst possible way.

Feedback, radical candour and critique are tricky to do well, and often end up looking like the inoffensive and yet desperately offensive line on this man's screen. How have we reached a point where the most insightful comments a professional could hear have been condensed into this one-size-fits-all Post-it note? It is because, more and more, the deliverers fear the reaction of the receiver. From tears to blank expressions, to tell-all ex-employee TikTok rants, the repercussions mean we're perfectly happy to hide behind a smorgasbord of vapid comments, leaving the perplexed other party to mistranslate the true meaning behind the message.

I have seen two extremes of this. At one end of the scale, I once worked with a company that didn't give a f**k how their employees reacted, almost to the point of making a sport of it. I was brought in by this industry giant to help give a selection of their staff presentation-skills coaching, with a heavy emphasis on 'building resilience', a clue that I should have read into a lot further than I did. One by one, each tearful employee came to see me, each launching into a thousand very specific reasons why they were the worst communicator in their company, and possibly the world. The longer the list of reasons, the more I was convinced the speaker was not the problem. It transpired that each of them was required to give just three presentations throughout the course of the year, with no other opportunity to deliver outside these specific occasions. Against my ethos of 'public speaking is never a test', these presentations were exactly that. An opportunity for each speaker to 'defend' and explain the work they'd been doing in an allocated time slot. They could expect to be interrupted, challenged and have their points torn apart. One of them described it as 'being sent to the headmaster's office'.

The impact of these extraordinary events was that in the run-up to each presentation, speakers would experience insomnia and headaches and would fall out with their family. Once it was over, and they'd come to accept the seemingly unending lists of negative feedback, there was a brief period of respite where they could transform back into themselves, before it would start all over again. Many of them had been reduced to nervous wrecks, able only to read off a watertight script while clicking endlessly through complex slides, put together painstakingly by their team. They were wasting time, money and resources, and most of the employees half fantasised about and half feared being fired.

So why were they doing it? This company held a firm belief that pressure created performance and, to a large extent, it was right. In an environment where revenue generation was paramount to the success of the business, the harder they drove employees towards sky-high targets, the further ahead of their competitors they'd be, which would result in lovely, chunky bonuses all round. As they saw it, this was just part of the deal. As I saw it, it was a deal that came with some unexpected side-effects: employees walking around on a knife edge, who'd jump out of their skins as soon as the word 'feedback' was mentioned. *Harvard Business Review* has run studies that concluded that companies with effective feedback systems have 14.9 per cent lower turnover rates than those without. On top of that, Gallup, a renowned research and consultancy firm, conducted a piece of research that revealed that employees who received little to no feedback are three times more likely to be disengaged with their work than those who receive consistent and timely feedback. Think how much avoiding a difficult conversation could end up costing an organisation.

At the other end of this scale was a cheerful creative company that prided itself on how nice it was to its employees. When working with them, I was told that its ethos was to make each staff member feel truly valued, which they implemented by ensuring that no one was ever made to do anything they felt uncomfortable doing. This was problematic, given that public speaking is very much at the higher end of 'things that feel uncomfortable'. Open and honest feedback was put into the same category, meaning that no one ever said anything to anyone that wasn't very enthusiastic praise. The greatest fear in the company was not that they might miss crucial targets or revenue but that someone should walk out of the building feeling upset or offended.

The most extraordinary example of this was passed back to me in an anecdote regarding a training day they'd run on time management. Their overly relaxed approach to scheduling meant they had a huge problem with staff turning up late to work, and so, not wanting to address the issue directly, they'd run a workshop, 'guaranteed to improve the time-management skills of each attendee'. It started to fall apart after the first hour of the session, when most of them returned from the break late, including one woman who turned up twenty minutes after the session had restarted. The facilitator tried to demonstrate 'how to hold someone accountable' by gently asking the latecomer to explain her delay to the rest of the group. She refused to, and promptly walked out of the session in tears, reporting to HR that this incident had made her feel uncomfortable. A couple of other attendees followed her in support. Lateness continued to be a major issue.

The upshot of this incredibly supportive style of management was that they had an extremely low staff turnover, but they also had a very low promotion rate, meaning that just a handful of very stressed people at the top did the majority of the heavy lifting, with a large team underneath them who struggled to work proactively. Clients were leaving rapidly, and the sense of resentment in the air was so thick that it clung to every faux fur cushion in the 'well-being room'.

Obviously, between these extreme examples there is a middle ground. But rather than finding a balance between tyrannical and soft 'n' cuddly, take the approach that feedback comes down to one crucial factor: total belief in the other person. The belief that they could be better, the belief that they can be challenged, and the belief that they have the ability to change. If the other person can see how much you're on their side, they'll not only listen to the feedback you have, but they'll want to implement it, quickly. With an 'I want you to win' mindset, even the most sensitive or reactive people can grow, as long as the feedback they're presented with shows you stand with them, not against them. 'Try to be more confident!' shows that you're standing neither with nor against them but that you're not even willing to stand on the same planet.

Create an environment where people feel they can talk openly and candidly, and you'll find they feel more comfortable in sharing ideas, thoughts and concerns. But it starts with you: the more you push your voice forward and speak up, the easier it becomes for you and everyone else around you. Consistently and sincerely praise good work when you see it and jump in to intervene whenever you sense the other party is going in the wrong direction, and you'll reduce the number of difficult conversations you need to have over the course of your lifetime. Prevention is always, always, better than cure. Brief conversations held regularly will prevent longer, more uncomfortable conversations from happening down the line.

Feedback is one of the most essential components of trust and trust leads to 'psychological safety'. Dr Amy Edmondson is the Harvard Business School professor who is credited with the coining this phrase, which she defines as 'a belief that one will not be punished for speaking up with ideas, questions, concerns or mistakes'. Simply referred to as 'Edmondson Theory', it posits that team members who trust and respect one another are more likely to communicate openly, take risks and perform better. A team such as this feels more empowered to collaborate, share ideas and, in turn, offer feedback. That's why the last time someone asked you for an honest opinion on something, they might have encouraged you to be candid by saying, 'Go on, I trust you.'

When it comes to giving feedback, you should ensure that two things happen between you and the other party:

1   They believe you.
2   They know what to do with it.

How to Give Feedback to Improve

Let's say you have a team member who's usually great at what they do, but recently they're cutting corners, and the quality of their work has slipped below what you'd expect it to be. They've lost focus, and they're no longer the dedicated and passionate employee that they used to be. In fact, you've had a couple of client meetings where they've expressed the same observation. You know they're capable of more. How do you intervene?

Step 1. Prepare what you're going to say. Stick to the following format: *Evidence, Impact, Change*.

Evidence: Start by clearly identifying the problem or problems. Then look at the tangible evidence you can use to back up each issue. Use language that puts facts ahead of feelings. For example, 'I just feel like you're unmotivated and lazy' doesn't help. Instead, say:

I've observed that for our last three projects, your quality of work has dropped. I've had feedback from our clients to say they've had to step in and correct errors.

Impact: Next, define the impact of the action so that they understand the knock-on effect:

The problem with that is it means the client is unhappy, which reflects badly on us and means they're unlikely to use our services again, which is obviously a big issue.

Change: After that, describe what it might look like if this issue changed. Take this opportunity to recognise what they're doing well and express how good their future could be if they were willing to make the change.

I know you have a lot on your plate right now and, in the past, you've worked hard even when we're under pressure. If you could return to performing at the standard we expect of you, we can win back those clients, and you'll really start to shine in your role.

Alternatively, if this conversation reveals that it's not their level of input that's changed but the level of work that they've had to take on due to an especially busy period, the conversation might sound more like this:

I know you have a lot on your plate right now and, in the past, you've really worked hard even when we're under pressure. I want to offer you some extra support from our administration team, or even outsource some of this to a freelancer. That way, you can focus on what you're best at, and the quality of your work can return to the level that our clients expect.

Step 2: Deliver the feedback. Give the other person a heads-up first. Start with a question that indicates you want to discuss something. A simple 'Hey, do you have five minutes to talk about the client project?' will do. If they don't want to have the conversation there and then, ask them when they'd like to schedule it for.

Step 3: If you start to hear defensiveness from the other party, then give them space to ask questions. You can change the tone of the conversation or intervene by exploring how they're interpreting the feedback. Once you've taken the time to understand how what you're saying has landed with them, remind them that you're on their side, and you want to work with them to move to a positive change. Remember that they might react in a surprising or emotional way. The initial feeling that they show is unlikely to be the one they turn up with the next day. Even if they take it well, it's still important to take time to understand their side of things, so ask them questions too.

Step 4: Check for an understanding. Do not leave the room until both of you have agreed on the issue and the way forward.

Step 5: Set tangible targets together to keep them on track. Ask questions to confirm that they're clear on what they're going to do differently from the moment they leave the room. For example:

We're going to aim to correct these errors ourselves and then no more careless mistakes going forward. Can we agree to do that? Can you imagine anything stopping you?

Step 6: Check in to make sure they uphold their commitments. If not, intervene immediately.

How to Receive Feedback

Let's now flip that scenario. Imagine you are a dedicated and passionate employee, known for your high quality of work and attention to detail. Recently, though, you've struggled to maintain your usual standard of work because it seems as though more and more is being put on your plate. You feel you're having to compromise on quality to deal with the quantity. How do you ask for support?

Step 1: If you are not being given feedback on a regular basis, you deserve to hear it, so ask someone you trust for their candid thoughts as to how you could improve. Prepare and send questions in advance so it's easy for them to be specific and give examples.

Step 2: If you are given feedback and it doesn't land well with you, allow for an initial reaction, but try to keep cool. It's important that you stay objective. This is not an attack on your character; it's happening because the other party values you and believes you have potential.

Step 3: Questions are absolutely essential here. Don't be fobbed off with lines such as 'We need to see more dynamic synergy from you.' Ask for their definition of 'dynamic' or any words that could have an abstract meaning, and then contextualise them by asking for examples of what that change should look like, both before and after the change has been made.

Step 4: Put forward your own solution. Don't hesitate to ask for what you need in order for things to improve. If you've already started to think about remedies, it shows that you're not only aware of the problem but you're already proactively taking steps to amend it. For example, do you need more administrative support with a larger project? Could a mentor step in to guide the relationship with an unusually tricky client? Are there elements of your work that could be outsourced so that you're left to focus on the areas that you'll tackle with aplomb? Show you understand the solution just as well as you understand the problem, and the conversation will be especially productive.

Step 5: Do not leave that room without a crystal-clear mutual action plan. If you feel that you want to take the feedback away and then have a follow-up conversation once you've had time to formulate a response, then you should, but avoid defensiveness. If you can't get on top of your emotions, ask for a short break or reschedule.

The word 'feedback' has somehow ended up with a pretty unfair reputation. Tell anyone that you've prepared some feedback for them, and you can actually watch their soul depart from their body. Feedback is often seen as just the professional term for 'criticism', when in reality, it is a vital component for positive transformation. Chaos ensues when vague, smiley-face emoticons are used in place of genuine human expression or when the suffocating rigidity of unyielding performance metrics takes the place of a candid conversation. The ultimate goal of feedback isn't just for it to be delivered and heard with minimal pushback but that something meaningful comes of it. When given with the utmost belief in the other person's potential, it will always be useful.

If all else fails, just try to be more confident, yeah?

PART 5

ONE MORE THING . . .

19

I STILL CAN'T F**KING DO THIS

Here is the least interesting, most important story in this book.

It takes place at Gatwick Airport, North Terminal. It's a place where storytelling gets you nowhere, being too authentic might end up in a fight with customs, and convoluted, unsympathetic communication is obligatory, especially in the arrivals section.

Once again, the scanning machines were failing to detect anything in my passport that would identify me as a real person, let alone a British citizen, and so I was sent to queue up to talk to an actual border control officer. My place in the line was behind a large family of over-excited children, and in front of a slightly sunburned and pouty man wearing cargo shorts. Mr Cargo Shorts was making huffing and puffing noises, before he pulled out his phone and launched into a lengthy rant. Initially, I suspected he was recording a voice note that he'd later use in an angry customer-service email to be immediately filed under 'trash'. But he then signed off his message in a way that made me realise he was leaving a voice recording for someone he actually knew.

> ... Anyway, that's *my* trip so far. Completely unbearable. So frustrating. Can't believe I have to sit in this queue and now Gatwick is going to force me to miss my connecting flight. Absolutely ridiculous. You won't get this now, babe, you're probably well on your way. I would say 'see you there' but I seriously doubt I'll make it. So, *bye*.

I briefly wondered how his other half would feel about their relationship on listening back to that recording, before looking at the endless line of miserable faces ahead of me. Just as I noticed one of the small children try to attach a lollipop to the plastic barrier by licking both objects and pressing them together, there was a kerfuffle behind me. An Australian man with an enormous rucksack was bustling his way up from the back, and as opposed to being met with the white-hot hostility you'd expect from a group of queueing people (especially the English), the sea was parting for him. He stopped at Cargo Shorts Man, who made it quite clear that he was the last bastion of British values, and stood before him, silently, physically, demanding an explanation.

'Hiya, mate, look, I know this is, err, well look, basically, you gotta help me out. If I don't get through this queue I'm going to miss my connecting flight. Can I please go ahead of you?'

Cargo Shorts peered at the boarding card being proffered at him before not quite breaking out into a full smirk.

'We're on the same connecting flight. And I'm here. So.'

And he drew an invisible line by spreading out his hands, indicating that while the Aussie had made it an impressively long way through, he'd be going no further.

Then something interesting happened.

'You're on the same flight? Mate! Why didn't you say so! Come on, I'll take you with me.'

And suddenly, they were both off. I stepped back immediately, gesturing them through. The Aussie was begging, pleading, joking with the crowd to get them to the front in seconds, and he was communicating for both of them. He dipped into his spiel whenever it was needed, but this time adding in, 'And my buddy here, he's with me. You gotta help us out.'

His approach was shameless, resourceful and completely effective. I was so distracted by the sight of these two unlikely heroes sailing through Border Force, I had barely registered that the lollipop had now successfully been attached to my suitcase.

This banal story perfectly explains the choice we make whenever we choose not to say whatever it is we need to say, out of safety, fear of rejection, or shame. You can stay where you are, play it safe, let the resentment build and curse your gods for not blessing you with the ability to speak up, or you can take a chance and find yourself at the front of the queue.

Just ahead of you are opportunities that are so great you can't even begin to imagine them, and all you have to do is start talking. On top of that, becoming a fearless communicator means you'll bring others along with you on your way.

*

If you have come this far and still feel you can't face an audience of any kind, here is the tough love you need to hear. Because now, the only, final obstacle standing in your way is you. No matter how many books you've read like this one, you now need to take everything you've absorbed off the page and start to use it, every bloody day.

Of those two characters at Gatwick Airport, you can immediately tell which one is going to make it further in their journey and which one is happy to let a series of difficult events hold them back. I can tell from the second session which of my clients will radically transform because it's evidenced in the examples they bring me from the moments when I'm not there with them. They deliver these like a schoolchild who's been told to tip out the contents of their satchel onto a teacher's desk, waiting for me to find the contraband. What I see instead are the results of someone who is trying their hardest to implement tiny (or even enormous) changes, from the perfectionist who throws an impractical idea into the brainstorming session, to the CEO who boldly announces that they've ditched their 100-slide deck ahead of the next town-hall meeting.

The man in cargo shorts fears rejection. He feels beaten down by an invisible set of rules that keep him uncomfortably in his place, never realising that he might be the one in control of whether he makes it to his destination or not. But the bold Aussie has formed a different view – that while the world can occasionally work against you, he knows that every single person he's about to speak to will at some point in their lives be in the same position as he's currently in. This knowledge, combined with the acceptance that he might irritate a few people along the way, is what enables his 'fuck it – it's worth a try' attitude. He fundamentally understands that it's worth it for the opportunity in front of him. And there's that ethos again, that foundation that underpins every single sentence in this book: 'Care Less.'

Let's revisit what you need to have in place to metaphorically tattoo 'Care Less' across your heart:

1 Know You Know Your Shit.
2 Don't Aim for Mass Likability.
3 Try.

By now, these three mantras will have become ingrained, but it's the last of these that I ask my clients to focus on just before we part ways. This final step is the one they have to take on their own, unassisted – to try.

You must try. There's nothing stopping you. There's absolutely nothing stopping you from speaking up in your next meeting, smashing that speech or pushing back the next time you need to. Nothing physical is standing in your way, so ask yourself again what you're afraid of. Don't finish this last chapter assuming that you now magically have the ability to do any of this perfectly, or without fear, but if you can take this last piece of advice, you will see a change. Or you can continue to stand in the line, whinging and waiting inertly to miss your connecting flight. You only have a few pages left now. How do you make sure the moment you've closed this book you're going to take action?

Well, as this is your final session with me, it seems appropriate that we agree on some homework together. Go back to the front of the book and look at the list of chapters. Take a look at that list and pick one, just one chapter about something you would like to improve at. Revisit it and then think of the smallest possible step you could take to try it out in a way that feels safe. Once you've tried it, be as honest as possible with yourself about the results. If it goes well, identify what the next step will be. If not, go for it again. Above all, keep trying.

For example: if you want to get better at saying 'no' but can't even imagine saying 'no' to your boss about taking on extra work – yet – start by saying 'no' to the offer of an additional napkin at Pret.

If you want to get better at speaking up, but you can't speak up in the big meeting – yet – start by making one point in a small one.

If you want to get better at asking for what you want but can't ask for a pay rise – yet – start by asking the person you live with to do more washing up.

The one thing I hope you take from the book is that your audience is made up of human beings, with just as many needs, wants and worries as you have. At the start of this book, I spoke about my client listening to Taylor Swift to 'get into the zone', preparing to deliver the performance of a lifetime. But my job allows me to see the story from both sides, and following the audience home is the best way for me to understand how a single experience can be perceived in astonishingly different ways.

After I watched that client deliver his speech, I followed the people pouring out of the enormous stadium down into the tube station. Here's where I can scuttle about and listen to the actual feedback, where people say the sort of things they're not brave enough to tap out into the online form. I'm apprehensive as I lean in, but what I'm hearing is good. Moving from one buzzing group to another, I recognise my client's name being praised more than a few times. But they move on very quickly, which is frustrating because I want deeper insight. What did they make of the case study? Did any of the jokes go too far? Should there have been more pop-culture references? Was it light enough? Heavy enough? Months of tiny adjustments and readjustments, script changes, half pauses, the carefully practised raising of an eyebrow, all now boils down to the opinions formed in these casual conversations.

Just as the doors are about to close on the train, I nip through and find myself squeezed in among a group of smartly dressed women who are clearly halfway through their full dissection, but my arrival seems to have ground it to a halt. Why aren't they saying anything? Have I somehow given the game away? Can they see through my act? I'm desperate for them to keep chatting, so that I can solve that mystery – that final question that every speaker asks themselves – 'But what did they *really* think of me?' And so, with feigned warmth and relief I clumsily prompt them.

'What did you make of that then?'

There is a heavy pause, a strong indication that something important is being held back from me, before one of the women sucks in her lips, leans forward, and lets me in on the big secret.

'Well, obviously the speaker was brilliant. But lunch was a bit disappointing.'

BIBLIOGRAPHY

Introduction: How to Care Less

Hintz, E. S., 'The Fosbury Flop – A Game-Changing Technique', Smithsonian Institution (8 April 2021); https://invention.si.edu/fosbury-flop-game-changing-technique

1 The 'Con' of Confidence

Arnette, S. L., and T. F. Pettijohn II, 'The Effects of Posture on Self-Perceived Leadership', *International Journal of Business and Social Science*, vol. 3, no. 14 (2012); http://ijbssnet.com/journal/index/1395

University of South Australia, 'When You're Smiling, the Whole World Really Does Smile With You', *ScienceDaily*, 13 August 2020); https://www.sciencedaily.com/releases/2020/08/200813123608.htm

2 Kill That Voice in Your Head

Telford, O., *Cognitive Behavioural Therapy* (Vancouver: Pristine Publishing, 2020)

Plaford, Gary R., *Fight or Flight: The Ultimate Book for Understanding and Managing Stress* (Atlanta: LitFire Publishing, 2018)

3 A Presentation

Lourey, J., 'Classic Story Structures and What They Teach Us About Novel Plotting', Jane Friedman (2017); https://janefriedman.com/story-structure/

4 An Inspirational Talk

Piaget, J., *Play, Dreams and Imitation in Childhood* (New York: Routledge, 1951)

Robson, D., 'The Underdog's Surprising Appeal', *BBC Future* (4 August 2024); https://www.bbc.com/future/article/20240802-why-do-underdogs-in-sports-and-politics-gain-support

Rosling, H., 'Global Population Growth, Box by Box', TED, June 2010, https://www.ted.com/talks/hans_rosling_global_population_growth_box_by_box

'Bitcoin buried in Newport landfill', Wikipedia; https://en.wikipedia.org/wiki/Bitcoin_buried_in_Newport_landfill

5 An Interview

Heath, C., and D. Heath, *Made to Stick: Why Some Ideas Survive and Others Die* (New York: Random House, 2007)

6 A Q&A Session

'Miss Teen USA 2007 – South Carolina Answers a Question', YouTube, uploaded by IRamzayI, 24 August 2007; https://youtu.be/lj3iNxZ8Dww

'Miss Teen USA 2007 – South Carolina on Today show', YouTube, uploaded by IRamzayI', 28 August 2007; https://youtu.be/fQKNvPn3V-8?si=uMmxjQDSCjY4_QOh

7 A Meeting

Lusk, D., 'The Psychology of Kodak's Downfall', *Psychology Today* (12 August 2020); https://www.psychologytoday.com/us/blog/unnatural-selection/202008/the-psychology-kodak-s-downfall

Chen, R., '8 Insights on Leadership from GM CEO Mary Barra and the Wharton People Analytics Conference', The Wharton School (9 April 2018); https://www.wharton.upenn.edu/story/8-insights-leadership-gm-ceo-mary-barra-wharton-people-analytics-conference/

Spocchia, G., '"Walk out of a meeting": Elon Musk's six rules for staff resurfaces', *Independent* (28 April 2021); https://www.independent.co.uk/news/world/americas/elon-musk-staff-six-rules-b1838960.html

Janis, I. L., *Groupthink: Psychological Studies of Policy Decisions and Fiascoes* (Boston: Houghton Mifflin, 1982)

Hern, A., 'The Two-Pizza Rule and the Secret of Amazon's Success', *Guardian* (24 April 2018); https://www.theguardian.com/technology/2018/apr/24/the-two-pizza-rule-and-the-secret-of-amazons-success

8 A Creative Conversation

Fey, T., *Bossypants* (New York: Little, Brown and Company, 2011)

Price, D. A., *The Pixar Touch: The Making of a Company* (New York: Alfred A. Knopf, 2008)

Watkins, J., *The 100 Greatest Advertisements: Who Wrote Them and What They Did* (New York: Dover Publications, 1959)

10 A Networking Event

Sugawara, S. K., S. Tanaka, S. Okazaki, K. Watanabe, and N. Sadato, 'Social Rewards Enhance Offline Improvements in Motor Skill', *PLOS ONE*, vol. 7, no. 11 (2012); https://doi.org/10.1371/journal.pone.0048174

13 A F**k-Up

Milgram, S., *Obedience to Authority: An Experimental View* (New York: Harper & Row, 1974)

14 Communicating With Difficult Creatures

Sonner, M. W., and C. Wilcox, 'Forgiving and Forgetting: Public Support for Bill Clinton during the Lewinsky Scandal', *PS: Political Science and Politics*, vol. 32, no. 3 (1999); https://www.jstor.org/stable/420644

15 Asking for a Pay Rise

Berne, E., *Games People Play: The Psychology of Human Relationships* (New York: Grove Press, 1964)

Reich, J. W., and F. J. Infurna, *Perceived Control: Theory, Research, and Practice in the First 50 Years* (New York: Oxford University Press, 2016)

16 How to Say 'No'

Flynn, F. J., and V. K. B. Lake, 'If You Need Help, Just Ask: Underestimating Compliance with Direct Requests for Help', *Journal of Personality and Social Psychology*, vol. 95, no. 1 (2008); https://doi.org/10.1037/0022-3514.95.1.128

YouTube. 'The Power of Vulnerability | Brené Brown.' Filmed June 2010 at TEDxHouston. Video, https://www.ted.com/talks/brene_brown_the_power_of_vulnerability

17 How to Disagree

Aitkenhead, D., 'The G2 Interview: Robin Williams', *Guardian* (20 September 2010); https://www.theguardian.com/film/2010/sep/20/robin-williams-worlds-greatest-dad-alcohol-drugs

Smith, A., 'Steve Jobs Wanted Dell to Run Apple's Mac OS but PC CEO Said There Was "Zero Consumer Interest"', *The Independent* (7 October 2021); https://www.independent.co.uk/tech/steve-jobs-dell-pc-apple-mac-os-b1933906.html

Bomboy, S., 'The Supreme Court Decision That Saved Muhammad Ali's Boxing Career', *Constitution Daily* (4 June 2016); https://constitutioncenter.org/blog/alie28099s-supreme-court-decision-was-biggest-victory

Spradley, J. P., and D. W. McCurdy, *Conformity and Conflict: Readings in Cultural Anthropology* (Boston: Little, Brown and Company, 1971)

Wadford, L., 'Tennis: As Retirement Draws Near, Nadal Shares His Regrets', *Leading Sport* (24 October 2024); https://leading-sport.com/

tennis/tennis-as-retirement-draws-near-nadal-shares-his-regrets/4794/

18 How to Give Feedback

Gottman, J. M., *The Seven Principles for Making Marriage Work* (New York: Harmony Books, 1999)

Lewis, T., 'Science of "The Dress": Why We Confuse White & Gold with Blue & Black', *Live Science* (14 May 2015); https://www.livescience.com/50842-dress-debate-color-perception.html

Mahler, J., 'The White and Gold (No, Blue and Black!) Dress That Melted the Internet', *The New York Times* (27 February 2015); https://www.nytimes.com/2015/02/28/business/a-simple-question-about-a-dress-and-the-world-weighs-in.html

Wikipedia contributors, 'The dress,' *Wikipedia, The Free Encyclopedia*, https://en.wikipedia.org/w/index.php?title=The_dress&oldid=1260536790

YouTube. 'Colour and Vision by Anya Hurlbert'. Posted by Darwin College Lecture Series. Posted 25 April 2021. Video, https://youtu.be/r_JySaqXL2o?si=etl8KGfh4ESkSjeq

19 I Still Can't F**king Do This

Burris, E., B. Thomas, K. Sodhi, and D. Klinghoffer, 'Turn Employee Feedback into Action', *Harvard Business Review* (November–December 2024); https://hbr.org/2024/11/turn-employee-feedback-into-action

Gallo, A., 'What Is Psychological Safety?', *Harvard Business Review* (February 15, 2023); https://hbr.org/2023/02/what-is-psychological-safety

Gallup, *State of the Global Workplace 2024*. Washington, DC: Gallup, Inc. 2024. https://www.gallup.com/topic/employee-engagement.aspx

ACKNOWLEDGEMENTS

This book would have remained a mad fever dream were it not for a long list of brilliant people who turned it into the physical copy you have just finished reading. First and foremost, Charlie Viney, for being a brilliant agent, but more importantly, a lot of fun to drink with.

At Elliott and Thompson, Sarah Rigby, my dedicated and magnificent editor not only made the book possible, but readable, and Amy Greaves was the woman with the plan. Emma Rogers, who designed the excellent cover; Pippa Crane who had to deal with more grammatical errors than words; and Lorne Forsyth, who took me to lunch – I look forward to the next one. Thank you all for not even blinking at the title.

For Joshua 'Beaker' Viney and Kyra 'The Smiling Assassin' Cornwall, whose wedding was the catalyst for the whole publication, thank you for looking after your rat.

For professional guidance, huge thanks to Dr Elisabeth Carter, Coach Koroush Valiseh and General The Lord Dannatt, all of whom had excellent advice and astonishing levels of expertise. To two great leaders, Rob G and Cyrus C, thank you for imparting your wisdom and showing me the line between genius and insanity.

Ottilie and Adelaide, your fearless negotiation skills are inspirational.

ACKNOWLEDGEMENTS

For those friends who metaphorically and literally stayed up late with me, listening to chapters and then being brave enough to tell me what was working and what needed work, you are all a fine force for good. For Mackers, Chen and Greg, Corkie, Harry and Arch, and Raj and Eva, thank you to each and every one of you.

For Charles, who wanted to write his own acknowledgment, but was not allowed. I knew it was a goer from the moment you looked up from my screen and said, 'This is actually quite good.'

In East Anglia, Sarah Daines ensured that my clients remained happy and didn't go neglected during the writing process. I mean it when I say the empire would fall without you. For Dad, your obscure business advice is at last starting to come into its own, and for Mum, who not once in her life has ever failed to just f**king say it, thank you. Harry, sorry about the red trousers.

Finally, to each and every client I have ever worked with, I can no other answer make, but thanks, and thanks, and ever thanks.

ABOUT THE AUTHOR

Photograph by Nigel Davies

Susie Ashfield is the UK's leading speech coach. Over the last decade, she has helped industry leaders, corporate executives and public figures look good, sound good and feel great about public speaking. She has been extensively featured across the media and on numerous high-profile podcasts, alongside amassing over 1 million views on TikTok. She is a regular on the speaker circuit, having given talks on stages worldwide at FTSE 100 and Fortune 500 companies and at academic institutions from King's College London to the University of Cambridge. She lives in Notting Hill, London. *Just F**king Say It* is her first book.